A Marbled People, A Marbled Nation:

The Limits of Red and Blue

Mike Freeman

authorHOUSE™

1663 LIBERTY DRIVE, SUITE 200
BLOOMINGTON, INDIANA 47403
(800) 839-8640
WWW.AUTHORHOUSE.COM

First published by AuthorHouse 01/10/06

ISBN: 1-4208-9232-0(sc)

Printed in the United States of America
Bloomington, Indiana

This book is printed on acid-free paper.

Table of Contents

Chapter 1

Introduction

The 2000 presidential election exposed divisions in America that have subsequently widened, so much so that they've seemed nearly irreparable since. As deep, though, and seemingly palpable as these rifts are, they aren't renting the nation anything like what's reported in the press, a group given to the same sensationalism for which people as a whole have an inoperable weakness. Sensation, however, doesn't reach contagious levels unless it's rooted in facts, even if those facts are obscured by reckless speculation. People fleeing in panic from a flood warning, afterall, have their flight based in legitimacy, even if it's bloated by their own fears and emotions. It's the ones who honor that fear but keep their heads who end up filling the sandbags and moving what needs to be moved to higher ground. The current portrait of America in red and blue absolutes is no different, where the growing rancor in the nation along ideological fault lines is unquestionably real and must be heeded, but only after it's been stripped of the hysteria coloring it from extremists on both sides.

Simplicity has its place, but it has its limits, too. In the roles of pattern recognition and generalization it's quite vital in initially diagnosing a problem. Stopping at these first, easily discernible symptoms, however, tends to exacerbate rather than fix problems by insisting upon a rash solution to an immediate crisis where in fact neither existed in the first place. To truly understand an issue the employment of useful but limited generalizations must be further developed with the better suited tools of refinement and attention to detail. Doing so will see the world more for what it is - marbled and nuanced - than for what it's not - simple and absolute - and the means for level-headed rather than panicked solutions can be more readily had. The familiar maps of red and blue are a clear-cut example.

Again, to start, simplicity is useful. Political and ideological trends have undoubtedly magnified lately and seem to be slowly ossifying in specific geographic regions. In most instances, as well, these differing views are in obvious conflict. Additionally, if allowed to continue without attempting a reasoned, moderate reconciliation, these conflicts could conceivably turn into the crises that some people now think are imminent. They're not imminent, however, and the best way to prevent them from becoming so is to move beyond the initial use of painting the landscape in primary colors and seeing it for the mixture that it truly is. The home states of the 2004 presidential candidates - John Kerry and George Bush - are the best and only places that need a look in this light.

Massachusetts and Texas both earn their respective reputations as among the most liberal and conservative states in the country. Yet simply brush-stroking the one blue and the other red is helpful only in identifying electoral trends and obtaining a general feel of the majority political tendencies in both places. Beyond that it misses everything. A third of Texans voted for Kerry. A third of Massachusetts voted for Bush. One out of three may be paltry in an election, but it's an unquestionably significant portion of any population otherwise, and one that can't be dismissed. Texas, then, has the same percentage of blue within it as Massachusetts does red, and this can be said of every state, county, city, and village in the country to varying degrees. Forty percent of the South voted Democratic, for instance, while approximately the same percentage of New Yorkers and Californians went Republican. Looked at this way, the electoral maps become more complex - a necessary good. Indiana, staying in character, voted solidly Republican, or red, while to the west Illinois remained reliably blue. This doesn't mean, though, that everyone in Chicago is a big-government, socialist liberal or that every Hoosier is a war-mongering evangelical enamored with fiscal libertarianism. No individual anywhere, in fact, is all one thing or all another, and it's this that makes the nation as a whole a marbled one, because it's individuals - not counties and states - that make a country what it is.

Every person - no matter how steadfastly liberal or conservative they may appear - is tinted at least somewhat with swirls of the opposing ideology, and usually the discrepancies are much easier to see. Today the word 'liberal' - in the eyes of those opposed to it - is concomitant with the terms tax and spend, appeasement, environmentalist, pro-abortion, anti-gun, and atheist, or at least someone who doesn't firmly believe in a specific god. On the other hand, many people on the left - or Democrats - consider most Republicans to be impulsive war-touters blinded by an unthinking faith in Jesus Christ while not caring a lick what happens to the earth as long as there's money to be made. Stereotypes, then - in addition to being fun - are also effective when generalizing, and any given liberal or conservative so termed might fit one or more of these descriptions to an extreme degree. The usefulness, however, ends there. No one fills stereotypes completely, and most people - considering the current political climate of blue and red - are a balanced mixture of the two. This book is an attempt to prove that.

I can't speak for anyone but myself, and so in several essays have laid out my personal beliefs in regard to many of the social, political, and economic issues currently dominating the country. Doing so, I hope, will accomplish several things, high among them proving that no one is all liberal or all conservative, and the two terms in fact have severe limitations when it comes to labeling an individual. Generally speaking, I'd be considered liberal by most broad definitions. Though I live in Alaska now, I grew up in Connecticut and in many ways fit the mold of a New England lefty. I'm for national health care, heavily pro-environment, and would like to see public education funding both expanded and spread out equally. Yet underpinning these decisions and others there are what many would consider conservative foundations. I'm pro-choice, for instance, but understand that an abortion is terminating a human life, or at least the start of one. Globalization, I believe, and its insistence on unregulated free markets is a perilous step backwards, but I think if we're going to do it we may as well do it entirely. I was against the Iraq invasion from the beginning. Again, though, much of this is largely based on what not long ago were considered core conservative principles. Conversely, I'm also very much pro-gun, but it's a belief founded more on liberal dogma than anything else.

It's hoped that these essays will reveal the marbling of all individuals. I consider myself wholly average, in other words, and wish to show people with a rightward lean that they have more in common with those on the left than they realize, and point out to mostly left-thinking people that a liberal vote doesn't necessarily spring from purely liberal thought. While I've been unabashedly disappointed with George W. Bush, I acknowledge what I think he's done well, trying in other places to lay out clearly the direction I'd like the country to head. I've voted mostly Democratic in the past, but the parties are currently in transition, in many cases switching roles in recent years. Like most people, I'll vote for the candidates nearest in line with my own desires, conceding the fact that no party can ever make one person entirely happy, a reflection upon the diverse tinctures that make up each one of us and therefore the country.

Chapter 2

The Price of Victory

Instinct means everything to most people most of the time. What our guts initially tell us - whether right or wrong - is often our enduring opinion on the matter. Ever since he became known nationally I've never liked George W. Bush. Cocky, loud, crass, shot-through with an air of entitlement, I simply didn't like the feel of him, and we tend to move away from people who put us off viscerally. Whether we can finger that irritation or not doesn't make the feeling go away, so when the 2000 election finally came to an end I was obviously disappointed, even bitterly so. However, like most of the country, the mere length of that process made me glad simply to have resolution. By the time Bush was sworn in, I was ready to shelve my instincts to see what the guy could do. He started with a flourish.

For generations the Republican party made no pretense of racial integration. They were, in fact, against it. The Democrats made motions towards and even several inroads upon discrimination, but to hang on to the South they had to tread lightly. There is, of course, some truth to the charge that liberals merely wrapped a few legislative scraps in maudlin sentiment and tossed them towards blacks to secure their electoral power, but by and large an earnest sense of injustice was the motive, and this culminated in 1964 when Lyndon Johnson abandoned the white South for Civil Rights. Though two generations later the

Republican party is still enjoying those repercussions on election days, the grander ripples of the sixties' transformation have seen - if not a sea change - at least a weakening of the entrenched racial prejudice that has characterized this country North and South since its inception. These positive movements were never more palpable than when George Bush, a Republican president and a southerner, picked his cabinet in 2001.

It's not that I liked his picks. Rod Paige, Colin Powell, and Condoleeza Rice may be fine people personally. If I knew them privately I may have even made good friends of them. Unfortunately, in a country of two-hundred and eighty million, voters rarely if ever know public servants in the flesh, elected or no. We're acquainted through their politics and polished television performances and our judgements are based on these alone. Though I knew Powell a little through the Gulf War, it was mainly as a soldier, and Rice and Paige I'd never heard of. Like a lot of voters when presidents pick cabinets, I found out what I could of these people, and apart from interesting personal stories I didn't like much of what I found.

Powell had too much blind loyalty in him. This makes for fantastic squad leaders but to me a secretary of state needs to voice dissent if he or she sees fit. Paige is gone now and I never got to know him well, but from the outset I thought his religious fervor a little forceful for public office, especially as the head of education. Rice downright gave me the creeps, and still does. Much like Bush himself, I couldn't locate what exactly was troubling, but something was amiss. Whatever it was I knew it to be the opposite of her new boss's flaws, or at least flaws as I saw them. Where Bush is outlandish, there's something sinister about Rice. She lurks. She obviously has brilliance but it seems tilted the wrong way. Rarely center stage or even quoted much, she still seems prominent, skinking about Bush like Iago about Othello. From what I could gather she, too, possessed a religious zeal that in my opinion might taint her new post with a color unbecoming of a government largely freed from dogmatic influence. Background-wise, her deep roots in the oil industry worried me as well, but that one I let go, as lobbyists of all stripes find cabinet posts in every administration. Resource conservationists have to put up with fossil fuel promoters in certain cabinets as much as oil champions must tolerate solar advocates in others. Sometimes democracy tips your way, sometimes it doesn't.

It would be both foolish and a lie to say I didn't notice these three appointees were black. You can't help notice someone's color any more than their sex. But I did notice that it didn't matter, not a lick. Not once as I privately vetted these people did it ever occur to me that Bush picked them as mere conciliatory tokens, as has been a much validated charge against socially conservative politicians since Reconstruction. He chose them because they were well qualified and in his mind the best people for the job. I believed that then, and as vehemently as I disagree with most of Bush's decisions at home and abroad since, I believe that today. That I still oppose his picks doesn't mean in any way I oppose his motives, and that's as true of his 2005 Hispanic nominees as it was of Powell, Rice, and Paige.

This is a giant stride forward, for as diminutive as my input may be, I didn't hear much nationally about race concerning the Bush cabinet, either early or later on. When it was clear Powell was going to tout Bush's Iraq invasion publicly while suppressing private reservations, Harry Belafonte did call him a house slave, and amidst the expected Democratic vitriol following the 2004 election, a media figure un-equivocally called Rice Aunt Jemima. As unfortunate as these barbs are, they seem somehow paltry when matching three high ranking cabinet members against the nation's overall history. A hundred and forty years ago slavery was legal. While in some regards that's a long time, it's less than two average life-spans, which culturally speaking isn't long at all. In addition, blacks were still publicly lynched through the mid-fifties, when my own father was in high school. Lastly, it's only a little facetious to say that outside the army and floor level factory work blacks through about the seventies had few prospects professionally beyond a craps table. Then there's segregation. I was born in 1968. Diners weren't desegregated in some towns as far north as Lancaster, Pennsylvania until that same year.

As bitter, then, as the Jemima and house slave comments are, they seem a grain of salt in an old - if not quite healed - wound, given the high-level national influence Rice, Powell, and Paige had during Bush's first term. The irony, of course, is that these words were issued by liber-als. Belafonte, I suppose, was granted a pass since he's himself black. The Jemima cat-caller, being white, left an uglier stain. Regardless, both comments had the same implication - that these people had sold out, becoming vassals of the very party that held them down for so long.

This couldn't be more wrong. From abolition to nixing poll taxes to Brown vs. Board to Civil Rights, the whole point was to ostensibly elevate blacks both legislatively and off the books - in people's minds - to the point where each person could realize their own individuality without being jammed in a racial box. Legislatively we're there. Off the books we're not, but we're much closer than we were thirty years ago and leagues away from the ambient state following manumission. Blacks may have thought and voted more liberally in the thirties and forties, say, simply because it was in their best interest to do so, as white attitudes restricted them to tight professional and social bounds. Even if a black woman in the sixties was against abortion, wanted low taxes, and had concerns over the secularization of schools, she most likely would've voted Democratic simply because that was the party fighting to emancipate her true self from economic and cultural oppression. If that day hasn't come, it's very close. Colin Powell, Rod Paige, and Condoleeza Rice are all by nature conservative people, as that term is now defined. They're for low taxes, high spending, violent aggression abroad, and a shift back to where religion plays a more embedded role in our public life. On the one hand, these views infuriate me. On the other, I'm elated that as blacks these three are able - in my lifetime - to not only freely express their inmost selves but to advise a president who shares their views, and who chose them for that reason alone. Nationally, this is a great victory. For the Democrats and the Republicans who made it possible in the sixties it seems their labor has borne at least some fruit, if not a full harvest. For the current Democratic party, however, it's a victory that comes with a political price. It's a price, though, that should be welcomed with glory rather than penny-ante vindictiveness. There's plenty of other wars to be fought.

Chapter 3

Exposure

I was against the Iraq War from the start. Everything about it reeked. Though I believe the ideal of democracy in the Middle East a meritorious one, I thought this particular approach laid out George Bush's character impediments specifically and America's by way of reflection. Rash, harried, and stitched together, the justifications showcased both Bush's petulance and the dissembling panic often generated by the current Republican party, an emotion used to thrust public opinion to critical mass. It worked, but the predictable backlash following Baghdad's fall scuppered the foolish notion of the Iraqis' eagerness to receive us, and if nothing else revealed the current administration to be either invidious sophists or grossly incompetent. Either way, it's an ugly fiduciary severance between a commander-in-chief and his line soldiers. Very well. The fact now is that we're at war and must work within the circumstances to produce the best possible result for the world, and inadvertently I believe the conflict has forced a critical institution, the United Nations, to tack that way.

If you rationalize nimbly enough you can see the positive backslides of history's most egregious acts. Sometimes these offshoots are intended, sometimes not. America's framers are rightly maligned for addressing slavery with silence. This produced another seventy-five years of bitter bondage, a ruinous civil war, and generations of racial discord that lurk today. Their intention, though, was America itself. They knew the union would dissolve if they confronted slavery at that time and they were right. Subsequently, if looking for a positive, their abstinence gave the world America, and in terms of ideals and theory I believe that's been an exponential good, if the country itself hasn't always been so. The obvious positives of World War II, on the other hand, are up front - fascism and Biblical brutality were crushed. Once these malignancies were launched, however, their stoppage, at the risk of unspeakable consequences, was a foregone conclusion. The trick is finding a positive in Hitler's initiating the war in the first place. That's slippery, but it can be done. European history probably records more years of war than not. If nothing else Hitler's spur may have finally stimulated the continent as a whole that tearing each other to pieces every half generation is a bad idea. Outside the Balkans they've since enjoyed their longest peace on record. For the price of fifty million dead sixty years isn't much, but it is something. Conversely, Bush's war, if it doesn't produce centrifugal catastrophe, has already turned up one positive that if exploited could fortify world stability for generations.

One strength of the Republican party over the last couple decades has been its distrust of the UN. Though I don't agree with those who want it abolished, I do appreciate the ability of their loathing to see the UN for what it is - a weak, corrupt institution. I want the UN. Rectified, it will serve the world the way a strong central government serves America. People like John Adams and Alexander Hamilton knew what the anti-Federalists didn't - that states rights would serve a vital function in the new union, but if they circumscribed the influence of centralized power cracks would inevitably form. These fissures would in turn be exploited by outside interests and the country would shatter. The federalists won, and though ever since America battles with how authority should be delegated, very few people today - the Bush administration especially - dispute the value of central primacy.

The world itself didn't need a central power then. Correspondence and transport took up to months to cross oceans and continents, and the globe seemed what it in fact was - vast. Technology, however, has expedited commerce to the point that current countries are like the newfound states of America's origins - they'll do far better with a strong central power that can react with speed and authority when mediating the age-old conflicts over resources, territory, and religion. Right now the UN is a poor substitute. Crippled by torpid bureaucracy and delegates from cultures that don't yet understand each other, the institution has been wracked with sluggishness, graft, and ineffectiveness. Bush's people recognized this, and nowhere has the UN's ineptitude been more glaring than in the United States' invasion of Iraq. I doubt this was intended. Of all the motives put forward for Bush's decision, exposing the debilities of the United Nations is not among them. It is, though, an unforeseen consequence, and now that the thing's been done the world should move quickly to purify the one institution with the best chance to peacefully arbitrate future incendiary disputes.

The Iraq War proved two things specifically - that the UN doesn't have the dexterity required to prevent preventable wars, and, perhaps linked, the graft that by now has proven rife. A strong, agile, globally centered power represented by all nations and gifted in jurisprudence would've stopped the United States from moving on Iraq. Unfortunately, America has assumed these qualities for itself, with which we've arrogated to our government the right to pre-emption. The UN - slow to move, embroiled in the Oil-for-Food bribes that may be the governing motive for their feeble performance - failed miserably here. Had they been the judge the world desperately needs they would've been more forceful with both Iraq and the U.S. - as well as hearing all other interests - and brought the disputes to a reasonable compromise. Neither country, however, gave UN authority the credence it needs for operative respect and war resulted, with the regrettable result that one country - America - currently dictates global powers better suited to an able, representative central block. This would be identical to Virginia alone lording over the rest of the states during America's first years, a strength it may well have had at that time. Inevitably, however, those states would've eventually galvanized, with the result decidedly not in Virginia's favor.

How the Iraq War will turn out is unknown. The early 2005 election was encouraging. It may be that democracy will eventually flourish and be taken up across the region. If so, George Bush deserves all the credit. Failing this, though, he should - whether he intended it or not - be praised for revealing the United Nations' perilous weaknesses and the attendant realization that an effective central body is earnestly needed to govern the now intensely compacted world. The United States would be the primary beneficiary of such a power.

Chapter 4

The Anti-Christ

Sometimes the new issues are the old issues. In the 2004 election components such as environmental policy and economic disparity revolved around a foreign war with imperial overtones. In kind, the 1902 election centered on the environment, class division, and a controversial, imperial war. Of all our persistent dilemmas, however, nothing's hounded us like immigration, if for no other reason than that outside a tiny percentage of natives we're all immigrants, or at least the descendants of such, which makes most opponents of the process - no matter how ardent - at least a little leery of themselves when wanting to raise the draw-bridge. Besides, since its inception America has always benefited from a healthy glut of newcomers willing to do any job for any price, and this is particularly true if we're to stay even remotely competitive in the modern free market. There are, though, several glaring factors that currently make immigration a more touchy subject than even the heady days of dagos, micks, and the Yellow Peril. While this is particularly true in California, Arizona, New Mexico, Texas, and Florida - over half the needed electoral votes in other words - it deeply affects the whole country. We can, then, do one of two things - something or nothing. Like a rising majority - including many first and second generation Mexican-Americans - I'm with doing something. There are several options and various combinations, however, and as in all compromises the idea is to give both sides the most of what they want. Fortunately, America has always had a gift for both compromise and assimilation, and as the two countries - America and Mexico - become more and more diluted by each other's influence an agreement of some kind can unquestionably be had.

A look at who and how many are coming is needed first. That part's easy, for despite a steady in-flow of Africans and Asians in recent years, when we talk immigration these days we're talking Mexico. For generations Mexican culture has colored America for the better and Mexican labor has propped up our agriculture and therefore the whole country. These are still facts, though the exploding U.S. population during that time coupled with an exponential influx of recent Mexican immigrants has transformed a regional issue into a cross-border relationship that can no longer be avoided. This pairing is symbiotic to some while highly disjunctive to others, and though this has always been true along the border it's now pervasive by way of simple geometry. There's a lot more people in the country, in other words, and heaps more Mexican immigrants migrating than ever before. In addition, they're going to all corners of the nation in greater and greater numbers, causing a natural friction of its own. The reasons for this have remained relatively constant, but their order has changed. While racism still claims a cornerstone in this country it's no longer the center beam, and I believe it takes a remote third to crowding and job competition in regard to tension over Mexican migration. If competition has always been a problem, however, space is relatively new. In the 1800's, for instance, there was plenty of room to put the Irish, Germans, Italians, and Poles. This was true for most of the twentieth century, as well, and neither did the Jews, Japanese, Chinese, and early Mexicans have much trouble carving out some space for themselves. Though America currently still has hordes of open land, the best lots - along with most of the second, third, and fourth rate parcels - have now been taken. Link this to a host of decent-paying jobs being lost to cheap labor - such as stone-work and construction - and the problem compounds. Throw in the fact that this cheap labor has been fundamental in the recent housing boom and many other price-related bargains - from the restaurant industry to hotel service - and the issue gets even more interesting. The problem, then, has to be addressed, the only question is how.

On the other side of doing nothing are the recent efforts to blow immigration wide open. Granting immunity to most illegal aliens essentially makes for an all-permeable border. While this would certainly have benefits - such as cutting border control costs and creating a tremendous boon to businesses in search of cheap labor - it's not the way to go. This would crowd land even more and push a dangerous amount of people already living here further out of work. On the other hand, placing pill-boxes along the Rio Grande - as some people would have it - and blasting every jack-rabbit that comes across isn't exactly practical either. As always, then, a middle ground must be found, and there are several options.

Though I believe a stiffened border while things are being worked out is a good idea, the best solution is to first understand why people of any kind move from one place to another. In general it's a dove-tail of two factors - conditions in their homeland are anywhere from difficult to intolerable coupled with the fact that their destination has much more to offer. Corruption, exploitation, free trade, continued American farm subsidies, and an unstable economy have for years contributed to a tough Mexican job market. America, on the other hand, has loads of jobs, offered by employers constantly seeking to cut labor costs and supported - if tacitly - by a consumer base wanting cheaper services. While this may seem like exploitation on our part, that's true only when taken out of context, which means Mexican workers exploit the American labor market in their own turn. It's a simple fact that people wouldn't come here - leave their friends, family, and homeland in other words - if it wasn't worth their while. The idea, therefore, is to make the homeland a more job-friendly environment, because the truth is very few people want to leave the country of their birth if they're comfortable there.

To do that - to make Mexico a place where Mexicans can find satisfactory work - several steps can be taken. First and foremost America can move to end its enormous farm subsidy program, particularly to farms larger than family-sized. This would not only shore us up under the rules of free trade and bring government spending back into the stratosphere, it would go great lengths toward curbing immigration, even if only the seasonal variety. Mexican farms would then be level with American and therefore better able to compete on the world stage. Conversely, some American operations would go under. More land farmed there and less here means less movement across the border, particularly if the larger farms went down since they attract migrants in huge numbers.

Another option in the agricultural field would be to provide incentives for American laborers to work farms, somewhat similar if less robust than GI offerings. This would serve the country many ways, some concrete, some more abstract. Less measurable but equitable to hard numbers is the fact that increasing percentages in each generation nowadays have no connection with land. No matter how advanced our technology becomes we'll always need to cultivate land to produce food. It's vital, then, that we encourage as much of our population as possible to know something about either crop-growing, animal husbandry, or both. A tiny fraction would go into farming themselves, but if nothing else a healthy portion of the populace would regain a practical understanding of stewardship, knowing first hand that well-governed land is fundamental to a secure future. These incentives could take many forms. An extreme option would be to include farm work as part of mandatory national service, along with teaching, say, or the military. Personally, I'd be vehemently against this, as I believe the ability to choose your own way in life endemic to this country's greatness. A more favorable solution would be to offer college payments to young people as is currently done in the armed services. Each year worked on a farm would grant a pre-determined payment toward college expenses plus a modest stipend and health benefits while working. This would be bound to attract kids looking for tuition money who don't necessarily want to join the army, and every American working an orchard or tilling a field is one less slot for an immigrant. Combine this, then, with the legions of potential migrants who would remain home to work the re-juvenated Mexican farming industry, and the number of stay-at-homes would be substantial.

Farming, of course, isn't the only reason why people risk crossing the border. While agriculture may once have been the primary attractant, Mexican immigrants have now joined with cost-cutting business owners to make all-alien work crews a common sight across America. Construction, landscaping, masonry, painting - these and other once well-paying and desired trades have come to be more and more dominated by Mexican crews willing to work for less and without benefits of any kind. Manufacturing, as well, has suffered greatly, and while immigrant labor has taken away the jobs of natural citizens since America's origin, the numbers of people now coming in has elevated this issue to dramatic heights. Free trade - through things like GAT and NAFTA - is often the fingered culprit. Manufacturing has taken its lumps through out-sourcing, and on the surface it seems this would help natural citizens in areas such as masonry or construction. Less manufacturing jobs here means more people looking for blue-collar work, and more factories in developing lands like Mexico should mean more jobs there and therefore more incentive to stay at home to work them. Again, though, it must be remembered that people usually flow to where the money is. Jobs go over seas because the owners there pay them very little, and in Mexico very little is almost nothing since a peso is about a tenth of a dollar. Eight bucks an hour under the table laying brick in America beats twenty pesos an hour at a Mexican machine shop every time. One solution would be to annul GAT and NAFTA, and attempt to further thwart job flight by both penalizing companies for sending jobs to Mexico and erecting tariffs on Mexican products. This, though, would be a disaster from many angles. It would be outright economic war on Mexico for one, and additionally counter-intuitive to free trade as a whole, perhaps triggering similar border wars across the globe. If globalization has a prayer, it needs to be all or nothing. Something else, then, is needed, and the best plan - a union of the two countries - may seem at first like the anti-Christ to both places.

Most people laughed when the Europeans moved to make a con-glomerate of themselves. Not many years later, though, it looks like they've done a spectacular job. If they can somehow work with or around rising Islamic dissent, the rest of the kinks needing attention should be easily surmounted, leaving the EU a formidable economic influence. Being only two, the United States and Mexico would have a much simpler union, but one not entirely trouble-free. Mexicans would be rightly suspicious of American motives, fearing that they'd eventually cede much of their sovereignty to US interests. Americans, on the other hand, would have to be convinced that such a coupling would indeed do what it was intended to do - slow immigration to a trickle. While suspicions on either side may never be entirely quelled, immigration could all but vanish and Mexican sovereignty remain intact with a couple of simple tit-for-tats. If America would phase out its farm subsidy program, Mexico could reciprocate by moving toward a more balanced American model of business and labor relations. A minimum wage at least somewhat commensurate with that in America, for instance, in conjunction with health benefits and social security of some kind would greatly reduce the temptation of American manufacturers to locate in Mexico. To ease the expected transitional turbulence, the two countries would do well to adopt a single currency, making all expenses equal and greatly simplifying commerce between the new partners. The subsequent boons to Mexican agriculture and American manufacturing - along with a common exchange - would level things between the two nations, and Mexico, for one, would gain in many ways. Their farm output would increase manifold, and, equally important, they wouldn't lose the majority of their most energetic and innovative people to America. Finding comfort at home, these people would be more likely to start businesses in their own land rather than migrate to America where the incentives to do so would be either greatly reduced or completely nullified. For its own part, America would see the reduction or even elimination of immigration, and it would do so not through the unfriendly means of increased border security but by a natural process that would provide the most benefits to the most people on either side of the border. Whether such a partnering is feasible isn't the question, only if both populations are willing to now take mutually serving steps that in the past may have seemed like poison to each. One of America's most venerable mottoes is *y pluribus unum* - out of many, one. Faced with escalated difficulties on both sides of the border regarding immigration, Mexico and the US should adapt that phrase to the new world of globalization in order to steady themselves before things go too sour - *mojados y gringos, unidos.*

Chapter 5

The Physics of Christ

The Magnet

After the 2004 election it was made known that over eighty percent of Americans consider themselves Christian. That shocked me, not because I thought the count was high, but for the first time since I could remember I had to consider whether I was inside or outside that number. Filling out various forms and applications earlier in life I always checked 'Episcopalian' when asked about my faith. I never thought it odd that I hadn't once been inside either an Episcopal church or any other service apart from weddings and funerals. Though I've believed in some form of God or at least spiritual force my entire life, most times I've thought that power too remote for humans to ever fully consider, let alone exact. While theology within a religion vigorously debates certain specifics, belief demands precision when it comes to the actual deity. In short, I'd never been a Christian, but hadn't been forced to make that admission until recently, when the current alchemy of American politics and religiosity laid the question bare. It was a private *auto da fe*, and it felt like one.

I wasn't uncomfortable with the decision, and doubt I ever will be. Though my vision of the supernatural may be fluid my belief in it isn't, and I'm at ease with the uncertainty where it exists. I did, though, quite suddenly feel what is in fact true - that in terms of American culture, my native culture, I was marginalized in a very important way. The suddenness of realizing I wasn't Christian forced another question as well, or search rather, an internal quest, to see if I had any affiliation at all with Christianity. My surprise lay not with the results themselves but in the fact that what aspects of Christian belief I find appealing have been with me all my memorable life.

Actually, one I find not so much appealing as plausible. If I don't believe in demons and tridents specifically, I've always thought that ill behavior on earth is certainly atoned for in some form or another upon death. Like most people, my endpoint for human decrepitude is any crime against children, particularly rape and torture. That perpetrators of these crimes simply cease to exist when dead without ever having to suffer for the viciousness they exacted in life is if nothing else depressing. Whether it's the Christian Hell, some sort of Hindu karma, or a state in between I have no idea, but I'll never shake the notion that people are accountable to some form of justice beyond life for specific horrors they may commit while living it. Phrased that way, it's probably hope rather than any empirical plausibility that leads to that belief, shared in concept by the Christian majority around me. If hope, then, causes the one affiliation - that of atonement - it plays another role in the second overlap, solely that of attractant. I am, and always have been, drawn to the story of Jesus Christ, and more specifically to the hope provided in His beaten body drooping from the Cross. Given what it symbolizes, I don't know how anybody couldn't be.

Even for those most skeptical of Christ and Christianity there can be no denying both the figure's and the institution's ability to thrive. The most bitterly entrenched atheist must acknowledge that two-thousand years is impressive, and if Judaism's several millennia are added the awe is magnified. The original Christians survived three and a half centuries of persecution, while their ensuing Church went on to endure the East/West divide, centuries of bitter theological debate, the Great Schism, Martin Luther and the many who parted from him, Copernicus, Kepler, Galileo, the Thirty Years War, and, most recently and perhaps most astonishingly, Charles Darwin and the scientific onslaught that followed him. Today, in the midst of empirical evidence against it and a high standard of living sustained by a centuries'-old secular undercurrent, Christianity - though always fraught with faction - is enjoying its most dynamic global upsurge in generations. There's many reasons for this, many of them powerful, but only one is overarching - the symbol of the rood, or Christ on the Cross. Whether one believes the story of Jesus to be fact, fiction, or an admix of the two is irrelevant when discussing its power to draw. Judaism and Islam have both maintained themselves for great periods as well but by an large have held up through the power of ritual in established populations. Though Islam has gained its share of recent converts, nothing spreads itself like Christianity, and as all three - Christians, Muslims, Jews - derive from the same Old Testament origins, the power of Christian churches to pull people in must lie within their icon.

Like all venerated tales Christ's story has potent elements throughout. The nativity scene allures immediately, mixing specific detail, widely interpretative symbol, and paradox in all the right amounts. The intrigue continues as Jesus disappears at the age of twelve and stays gone until thirty-three. When He does re-surface, He goes on to deliver some of the most poignant, heart-felt, and easily understood philosophy in history, eventually drawing the sinister figures of power that any good story needs. These come in the form of conspiring Jewish leaders and Pontius Pilate himself, who wants to rid Rome of any troublesome inspiration for the grieving masses. Next is Judas' betrayal, a hasty, unjust trial, the enigmatic portrait of Mary Magdalene, and the brutal persecution of Christ himself. Independently these all have enduring potential. Together they're a masterpiece, but need a final, single image to bind up their collective power in a way that will permeate people from all cultures and social standing, and they get this in the crucifixion

The resonance of the rood, of course, begins with Christ's birth and culminates in his final suffering. This alone, though, while inspiring, is no way to propel a culturally pervasive religion and lifestyle through two-thousand years, even with the compassionate philosophy Jesus tendered near His end. Countless impoverished, oppressed people filled with decency have died wicked deaths at the hands of tyrants, and a tale needs much more if it's to command durable worship. It needs the supernatural, but more specifically an explicit answer to the troubling mysteries of life's meaning. If people are going to pay penance, they need to know their devotion will be rewarded, preferably in the terrifying unknowns of the afterlife. Nearly all religions - both dead and current - offer this in one form or another, but through the life and trials of Jesus Christ Christianity gives its followers something that other churches lack - God's willingness to suffer what humans suffer. Christian cohesion has fractured many times over whether Jesus was God Himself, His Son, or a mixture of the two, and these impassioned debates have led to violent ruptures in large part responsible for the Church's many offshoots. This, however, is immaterial at the most fundamental level, for every Christian believes Christ's story in some form, and this devotion understands that God incarnated Himself to endure the worst of human suffering executed by the ugliest aspects of our nature, and He did this in order to redeem the inherently corrupt human soul for salvation. This, then, is verifiable proof of God's love and kindness.

Unlike empiricists, who deny any supernatural force whatsoever for lack of proof, I understand faith. I understand it because I have it. That I can't give myself over to a specific religion only means I don't think humans capable of comprehending any specific aspect of a universal creator, let alone place themselves above everything else in the world by assigning it human form and character. There are times, however, when I fervently wish I could relent, and in particular relent to Christianity. In a small way simplicity plays a role here. Having one unshakeable model for the cosmos would simply make life easier. Though in large part I'm defined by speculating life's meaning and what God is or isn't, it can be a soul-wrenching affair and certainly takes up time. While it's largely constricting, then, in its own way faith in a single creed must be extremely liberating.

Beyond this, though, and more importantly, I envy Christians for the hope their faith provides, and for this reason I'm drawn directly to Jesus Christ. The Old Testament is one thing. Assuming unconditional faith that the Bible is the word of God, these more aged texts prove that He understands human suffering - both that inflicted by other people and the privations often caused by an indifferent natural world. Murder, intrigue, starvation, betrayal, plagues - everything to which humans are subject is included, and proves that God is truly omniscient regarding our earthly trials. To understand that others feel pain, however, is not to feel it yourself. Judaism stops short of the

New Testament, and while Islam confirms the brilliance of Christ, it denies His divinity. Only Christians go that far, believing that God sent either Himself or His Son to earth, to take on human flesh and therefore human suffering. He did this, according to the Gospels, to redeem mankind for original sin, but it's understood that He wanted to feel for Himself what humans feel when they suffer, and at the end of His life He truly felt the worst of it.

In itself the hope Christianity offers is staggering - everlasting life and reunion with everyone you loved on earth. More than that, though, there's the love of God. While He can be fearful, the love of the Christian God is unlike that of others, for through Jesus the Christian deity came to earth to endure the pains that all humans bear, perhaps as His punishment for our sins. In spite of these sins, however, He offers us grace, and He does so through the greatest love story ever told, by suffering through His own decision what we ourselves suffer. The rood is our reminder. His crushed body, dangling from the cross He Himself bore, tells us there's a God willing to sacrifice Himself to redeem our fallen state. For me that's Christ's magnetism, and the driving force behind Christianity's irrefutable pull. It's the most powerful single image humanity has yet produced. Still, though, I fall short, as to my sense of gravity there are agents in both this world and the next that pull much harder.

Free Radicals

Devotion to a single, structured worship requires several things, some of which I possess, others I undoubtedly lack, and one I hold in excess. Faith, the one force outstripping any other, I have in suits. To believe in something that lacks sensual proof defines faith, which requires a faith of its own - to trust in your intuition, your instincts. On earth this holds true in marriage. A wife can't know for sure what she can't see, nor can a husband. Spouses rely on faith, then, for their better's fidelity. When your wife's out of sight, instinct and intuition alone dictate whether your faith disintegrates or congeals. Conceptually this defines faith in the supernatural as well, whether it's in Jesus, Allah, Yahweh, Shiva, or extra-terrestrials. The difference, of course, is singular but vast. False faith on earth can be known. To put one's faith in a deity, however - which often entails a consuming adherence to certain rituals - means submitting to a power whose existence beyond human faith and conjuration may be null. This brand of faith is in another sphere - both literally and figuratively - from any trust we may hold on earth.

Christians obviously have faith in Christ. Each denomination has its variations and places more value on certain symbols and rituals over others, but the religion exists exclusively through faith in Jesus' verity. I understand this. In my own way I'm largely governed by faith in a creative power as well. My instincts are mostly titillated by the natural world, though, as I can barely look at a thing in nature and not have the sense that something - something forever unknown to me - played a role in its creation. Whether it's a tadpole, a monarch butterfly, a budding birch, or a chunk of granite is irrelevant. I'll never be convinced that either each piece of nature or the whole system webbed together - in all its creative destruction and destructive creation - came from absolutely nothing. What this force is or what role if any it plays in this life or the next I simply understand as beyond my reach. I do, though, have utter faith in its existence, and if the imagery is more distorted than a structured religion's and the framework more malleable, the intensity is no less certain. Since my access to this faith comes through the secular channels of nature it may be that its ethereal projections are more opaque. I don't know this, but I do know that through the vein of faith Christians and I have a common denominator.

But if we share faith in the abstract, we part cleanly regarding specifics. Adherents to Christ - along with most believers in a formal religion - know precisely what they believe. Everything from morality to images to timelines to biography is covered, laid out in stained glass or the written word. This gives their faith a rigid - if interpretively pliable - definition which I don't have. Whether it's in my soul, heart, or brain circuitry I'm not sure, but I decidedly lack or possess whatever's necessary to put faith in a structured, chronological religion of human time and form. Such conviction simply doesn't come, and there's reasons for this. With Christians I share a profound belief in humanity's embedded alloy, and though with humanists I'll always harbor an equal hope in our possibilities, my instincts are to regard human nature with suspicion. Christianity, then, with its progenitor Judaism, is a human religion. While it may be true that a humanly formed God did at one time speak to Moses, then returned many years later to save our souls with His suffering, both the reports and interpretations here were man-derived, as are the current institutions built around them. It's too cynical to say the world's great religions are founded on ghost stories, but on a certain irritable level that's true. Moses, the Gospels, Mohammed, and most recently Joseph Smith all in one way or another claimed they both spoke to and witnessed either God Himself, His messenger, or His son. One or all four may be true. They all occurred, however, with either a lone witness or in nebulous circumstances stitched together by human memory. All four have also produced immensely powerful institutions, and distrusting human power and motive as fervently as our nature at large, I can't help to suspect the beginnings of any dogmatic creed they may produce.

The matter of Christianity's human birth, though, is not enough in itself to knock me out of the fold. From the U.S. Constitution to the diesel engine to *War and Peace* the human mind has realized an infinitude of astonishing works and visions, both practical and inspiring. Many of the most admirable have even been abused by power. The toppling factor, then, in my abstinence from either the Christian Church or any other formal religion is actually a trait wholly necessary to those faiths but one I believe I hold in excess - humility.

Beyond the obvious differences of material and immaterial, known and unknown, visible and masked, there's a great gulf between secular and ethereal contemplation that for me reaches its depth in mood. To everything from the internal combustion engine to the fluctuation of free markets there's a wealth of human creation that I don't understand, and though this ignorance - even if it's beyond me intellectually - may be frustrating, it's never humbling, at least not as I define that emotion against the heft of God.

Like anyone, I've been humbled by earthly occurrences countless times. I've been cut low on football fields and baseball diamonds, made a fool of by crafty children and impish dogs, and been put to rest while arguing a host of topics, and love, of course, is another bad novel unto itself. To varying degrees all these have produced humility. None of them, however, in my experience, compare to the humbling effect instilled by the supernatural - more specifically what force created the universe and may or may not be responsible for our actions here on earth. Life's meaning and what happens after it are certainly included. This feeling can't be defined with the same word as those emotions engendered by secular sources, and I'm not sure human language quite has that word. This may explain the hushed atmosphere attending most churches. From English we can only precede humility with adjectives, such as 'crippling' or 'paralytic'. Most everyone knows the feeling, and many people are brought to their knees by it or even faint. At the very least, as with me, it can tear the air straight from your lungs.

People respond to the universe differently. For as many human beings who've ever lived there are that many shades of reflection. With nothing but our own sensual and visceral perceptions to guide us, questions that have no answers can be curious to some, terrifying to others, and quite peaceful to the ballasted few. Many people experience the gamut. Certainty is the prize in all these searches, a certainty that can never be verified in this life. This craving for exactitude, I believe, for some kind of stability in a universe of permeable boundaries and fluid definition, couples with an inherent human spirituality to produce our well-defined, structured religions. Comfort, familiarity, and superiority real or imagined go on to make most of these systems human-centered, and the divinely human figures that represent them, such as Christ, inculcate their believers with profound humility when these people are at their most inspired. As with faith, though, I veer from Christians here as well, in the route my own humbling takes when faced with the thought of God.

For me, what made and guides the universe is far too compound for human beings to grasp either individually or collectively. Since these matters most often seize me in nature, it's here I'm most familiar with their effect. Not always does the contemplation of God, death, and the universal secrets weaken a person; often I catch myself in the woods thinking of these puzzles with an unfrazzled, innocent curiosity. It's the unguarded moments, though, when you're most vulnerable. The size of the universe, its endlessness, humanity's puny conception of time in relation to what it may mean otherwise, the impossible paradox of our galaxy's perfect order striding aside utter chaos - when all these hit at once it diminishes me beyond deference, where it seems I've breached a contract, daring the complexities of God with nothing but a human mind. Hundreds of millions find comfort in Christ in these moments. I turn away, strongly, suppressed by a humility far too lowering to assume my own figure - my arms, legs, body, and head, even my mind - as kin to God's.

Divergent paths, then, in faith and humility will likely always prohibit me from Christianity, as urgently as I'm drawn to Christ in lore. These, of course - faith, humility, and lore - are elements we can neither touch nor see. This is to say nothing of what we do see on earth as it relates to Christ's story. That tale provides a hope like nothing else I know, but historically the present mirrors the past in most ways as far back as records are kept, including whatever fact or fiction makes up the Old Testament. Despite much elevation in our standards of living, medicine, comprehension of scientific laws, and some social movement - such as at least looking in the direction of racial and religious harmony - to this day people still rape, torture, abuse, swindle, and make war upon each other at rampant paces. Whether this validates the conception of evil or not is an open matter; the only fact we know is that we perpetuate apace the very viciousness that we're told Jesus recognized, suffered for, and ultimately died redeeming. That, then, may be the true comfort people find in Him - a divine rationalization to absolve any moral transgressions committed here on earth. That's too much for me. Moral behavior - while at times a monolith of ambiguity - is for the most part understood by all people at the principal level. Don't kill, don't lie, don't cheat, don't steal. These standards should be maintained because they're right, not for the incentive of salvation.

Many Christians don't begin life as Christians, or at least devoted Christians, but rather have an epiphany - usually at a low point in their lives - when the hope of Jesus and the structure of His worship enables conversion. That's possible with anyone, including myself. As far out as I can see, however, I'll remain apart from the overwhelming American majority regarding religion. Despite the power and comfort I take in Christ's great symbol of sacrifice and love, the chemistry of faith, humility, and interpretations of human behavior and morality simply mixes differently in me than it does in most Christians. If the riddles of life, death, God, and human suffering represent an ocean of mystery, then in Jesus Christ Christians see a bridge spanning that breadth. I see an ocean, and though at times the uncertainty is troubling, I have the confidence in my own lungs and limbs to plunge in and bob along with its fluctuations. This until I die myself, maybe to learn what lies in the depths, but for now to explore the surface where I have vision, for the most part comfortable with the uncertainty swirling around me.

Chapter 6

The Tulip Patch

Fringe candidates love abortion, or at least talking about it. From either the right or left people running three percent in the primaries fire at will. Abortion is either the device of Satan and outright murder or both a natural and Constitutional blessing up to and including nine months. As with all issues these candidates stand worry-free and serve to stir up the true believers on either side. That purpose is particularly graphic with reproductive rights, since for both office-seekers and office-holders abortion is the great tulip patch of American politics. No matter how firm an opinion one may have on the matter they best tread lightly when it comes to abortion. Bill Clinton could say he wanted it legal and rare but he couldn't say he advocated it. George W. Bush can state he wants to move toward a culture of life but he can't put "abortion" and "illegal" in the same sentence. Ginger steps are needed at all times and there's sound reasons for this, since unlike other temperamental issues - such as religion and guns - lives are directly at stake here, and not only lives but pre-natal lives. On the other side of it, people's lives - adult lives - are also at stake - their bodies, their futures, their living lives. Regardless of how it wavers in the courts, then, abortion in politics will never disappear, for at bottom lies the fundamental question of when life begins. It's one of our great mysteries, and we've been forced to make legal, secular decisions upon this ether ever since the U.S. Constitution collided with the immemorial practice of terminating a pregnancy.

I have my own opinion on abortion, though like the majority of us the topic unsettles me a bit. For many, though, it's easy. Pro-lifers simply define it as wrong. Some don't go so far as to call it murder or evil, but probably more out of a social sensitivity than anything else. Unrestricted pro-choicers, on the other hand, feel it should be legal for any reason at any time. Their passion is privacy, both biological and the right to choose one's way in the world. Passion is the key word here, as both extremes possess it in wild abundance, contributing to the uneasiness abortion instills in the remainder. This heightened emotion makes the topic devoid of nuance for its endmost opinion-holders. Pure pro-choicers see no life prior to birth and therefore a gross violation of personal freedom should that choice be taken away. Pro-lifers see life and life alone at conception, and to end life is indisputably to commit murder. There's no debate in either of these positions, which makes it similar to other topics, where extremists are in a scant minority. War, for instance, except for psychotic jingoists, is generally regarded the most regrettable policy choice, whereas only a few dedicated clans like the Amish won't concede that it's occasionally necessary. Nuance, then, plays a role everywhere but the outmost edges. It's the same with abortion. As one voter I can't do anything but form my own opinion, and since I reside in the nuanced majority I've done what is common and come up with a mixture.

I'm for abortion under three months and at any time for rape and incest. All political issues - from warfare to welfare to school vouchers - create a blend of visceral and intellectual debate within each individual. Abortion is no different but seems far more influenced by the gut than other issues. I have no idea when life begins, for instance, or why it begins, what God's judgement upon it is or if such a God and such a judgement even exist. Though I spend a great deal of time thinking about these things there's nothing intellectual to touch, so like many other people I rely on instinct. An undeveloped embryo being killed at two months by a woman just launching a career or a sixteen year old whose scarce half made-up herself is unappalling to me. Most women know they're pregnant within six weeks or so, and another six weeks should

30

be enough to weigh the extremely considerable decision of whether or not to give birth. Once the fetus develops and takes real human form, however, I can't help myself. For no tangible reason beyond physical queasiness the idea of sucking arms, legs, and a head out with a vacuum is revolting to me. That means nothing outside my own opinion, but it's a powerful influence inside that process.

Rape and incest, on the other hand, are an equally visceral topic. Women and girls who've experienced and become pregnant by these means shouldn't be expected to either come forth with the details right away or deliver the child of such occurrences for any reason. I don't know anything about statistics, but incest happens too often to be termed infrequent and rape is nearly as common as Sunday school in this country. Women do get pregnant this way, and to legally force a person to give birth under these circumstances is to tamper with evil every bit as much as those who say abortion in general tampers with it. I have no proof for any of this, it simply lives in my stomach and pulls its strings from there.

Where some aspects of an opinion, though, reside in the gut, others live in the heart. No one will deny that if life hadn't started before the first breath it certainly starts with it, and once a child is born to either an ambivalent or resentful mother the abortion issue takes another turn. While it's unquestionably true that any baby born has the chance of a healthy, happy life, unwanted pregnancies don't generally favor it. Poverty, neglect, and abuse most often lead to repetition in the ensuing adult, and the harried homes of dual working parents have contributed mightily to the dis-junction minds of so many kids today. This is not at all to say that a child born to wavering parents won't have a decent or even terrific life, it's just to state that the chances go down dramatically. Roughly speaking annual abortion numbers match those of reported child abuse cases. Assuming correctly that much abuse goes unreported, had those abortions not been performed then mistreatment of children would be more epidemic than it already is. Adoption, of course, is a viable and far more preferable option than abortion, but placing the million or so annually aborted pregnancies in good homes would be a tall order. It's a poetically pleasing irony that a great many gay couples would happily adopt a portion of these children, but that would put most pro-lifers in an awkward bind to say the least.

Regardless, gay folks wouldn't take them all, and as much as terminating an embryo may cut across our instinctual grain, the thought of so many more living, breathing children being born to neglect and abuse rends the heart that much more.

The head comes last, and though it's the most detached influence in decision making it's often the easiest to explain for that reason. For me, there are two intellectual rationales for maintaining abortion. As cold as these choices seem humans are often forced to make brittle decisions in both our personal and collective lives. In this case it comes down to population and economics. Nothing is more frigid than numbers, and both these entities consist of nothing but. There's a sound, inescapable economic tie to the more emotional side of adding a large number of poverty-stricken or otherwise abused children to the population. If even half these kids ended up indigent it would strain social welfare even more than it is now. It would also put a lot more kids in schools, where if people don't agree on anything else they agree that schools are too few and classes too large. Money, then, matters, and though by itself it's no reason to keep abortion legal it certainly lends support to that argument.

The second coldly calculating principle to ensure a woman's right to choose is population control. As it cuts against strong religious beliefs that place humans above animals in all ways, this one certainly appalls many people. Personally, of course, I value human life far higher than animal life when it comes to people living outside the womb. The test is simple. If you took ten thousand fanatical dog lovers and tossed their favorite pet in the surf, then did the same with a two-year old child whom they've never met and gave them time to save one, ten thousand people would save the child. Ten million would save the child. That, though, is instinct, a different value. Population control, however - though far more remote and less palatable - taps another instinct. Currently there are about 285 million people in the United States, quite a crowd from most viewpoints. In the thirty-two years since Roe vs. Wade about twenty million abortions have taken place, and the first generation of those would have been well into their breeding years by now. This would conservatively add about another two million, and numbers would compound from there. It's biological management, and it's simple. We champion the idea when it comes to culling deer herds and beaver crops but experience anything from surprise to utter horror if such a practice is mentioned in streamlining our own population. For me, though, as it fosters a healthier overall populace, it makes perfect sense. If terminating a million largely unwanted two-month embryos a year puts less strain on both our food supply and living space while lessening our risk of disease and warfare due to overcrowding than I'm all for it. It may be cold up front, but it's sound long-term.

There's one last trick to abortion. As a man I firmly believe my opinion can serve to advise on the matter but never settle it. If a woman ever became pregnant because of me I'd be horrified if she got an abortion without at least asking if I'd like to raise the child myself. The truth is, though, it's only my business to an extent. It's her body. She carries the baby and delivers it. Her chemistry, her figure, her emotions, and her life in general would all change and mine wouldn't. I could leave her. Men do it all the time. For this reason the decision of whether or not to deliver is ultimately hers. It should be no different policy-wise. Men, of course, should have an opinion - we certainly have views on abortion and they need to be heard. It is, however, a woman's issue in the end, and a mechanism should be set up where women and women alone conduct all legal debates regarding reproductive issues. This isn't a snap reaction against patriarchy or a quick out for a man to take, it simply makes the most sense to have a biologically biased issue be politically biased as well.

Though abortion's urgency in American politics will constantly be superceded by intermittent flare-ups from national security to the environment to farm bills, it will remain the most persistently divisive issue we have. With two large, deeply committed extremes battling for an uneasy middle majority, the topic confronts the impossibility of making earthly law from a spiritual question that can't be verified in this life. As much as I have my own private solutions for the matter, I sincerely hope Roe vs. Wade is overturned - not in favor of banning abortion but simply to acknowledge that no amount of rhetorical footwork within the Constitution can find either support or denial for ending a pregnancy. This debate lies outside that document, and it's there it must be held. Wherever the fight is fought, however, it will always involve more passion than reason, and it's this fact that will have even the most devout future candidates admonishing their God every campaign season for forcing them to tip-toe through this great flower patch of American life.

Chapter 7

Bushie the Goatfoot

Whether it's Karl Rove, Paul Wolfowitz, or George Bush himself I don't know, but someone in the Republican party studies ancient Greece. Pan, one of many gods and a goat-footed, half-human figure, puffed his magic lute in frightful ways in order to instill hysteria, forcing crowds to flee in a given direction. We get 'panic' from this, and at some point the Bushies clearly lifted it from the Olympus playbook. It's both a lethal technique in willing people your way and a great misfortune that fear can generate such well-meaning but misplaced vigor within groups of otherwise rational beings. Cut-and-dry legerdemain, this ploy is nonetheless brutally persuasive and something the American populace needs to ferret from the current political atmosphere. Even when pressed, deliberation and compromise are the country's true strengths and it's these that must regain leverage before we're knocked askant again by these piped-in fits of fright.

This particular panic device swayed popular opinion before the Iraq invasion, and it's been deployed mightily in the rush to push preset Social Security reforms through Congress. Legend has it, however, that the Bushies cut their teeth on this smoke-screening during the president's rise to the Texas governorship and then again in his march to the White House. Ann Richards felt it first, or at least its effects. Richards, then governor of Texas and an unmarried woman, became the target of 'whispering', the simple, devious technique of spreading rumors without those rumors ever being sourced. Karl Rove perfected it, or that's the hear-say, and in Richards' case it advantaged homophobia. As a single, somewhat aged woman it wasn't difficult to at least plant the possibility of lesbianism, which spread through Texas quietly but pervasively. This alone may not have swung the election, but it certainly played a part.

John McCain felt it next. His defeat of Bush in the 2000 New Hampshire primary made him a dangerous man. South Carolina held the next vote, and while hysteria didn't rage through the state suspicion certainly did. McCain and his wife adopted a Bangladeshi girl. Bush's camp used this fact to 'push-poll' potential voters. Not identifying their affiliation, campaign employees called people at home to ask questions about the upcoming primary. Among the inquiries was whether or not a man who had fathered a bastard, mixed-race child was fit to be president. Again, this may or may not have won an election, but it must've raised doubts about McCain in at least some minds.

Election year trickery, of course, is nothing new in American politics, and it can even be said that warping certain contextual facts - like being single or adopting a child not of your race - to fit rumors of lesbianism and lechery is scarcely a misdemeanor in the unfortunate but entertaining art of smear tactics. The fact that the Richards and McCain rumors were a little dirty is lamentable, but public figures expect to get roughed up during campaigns. Iraq, however, is different. Justified or not warfare kills people in great numbers, many if not most of which don't necessarily deserve it. In a case like Iraq America's technical superiority - particularly from the air - made high civilian casualties inevitable despite the sincere and often noble efforts to avoid them. Any Iraqis who wish to oppose this same superiority are nearly compelled to wage a guerilla war, which they of course did. Guerilla wars, if they're to be effective, are ugly and almost always involve terrifying and often executing civilians who don't support the insurgency. The deep South during the Revolution furbishes a similar if not so extreme example. All this should have been calculated which would've made the war what war should always be - the absolute last choice considered. It wasn't, though, and the death toll on both sides has been regrettable.

I'll give Bush some room on motive. It's probably true that a few small but influential lobbyists in the oil industry wanted the war simply so they could set up shop. I don't doubt this for a minute, but it shouldn't surprise anyone. Profiteers know battlefields the way prostitutes do - there's money to be made as long as you stay out of artillery range. For this reason business interests and whores have advocated warfare since apes threw rocks at one another. Bush, though, didn't go to war to make his friends rich. Oil of course is still the over-riding reason why anyone in the West cares what happens in the Middle East, and it's certainly plausible that the war was launched solely to secure fuel for the American economy. Jimmy Carter came up with the idea nearly thirty years ago, and in its humanly detached way it's sound policy. It's also entirely possible that Bush and those under him sincerely felt the suffering of the Iraqi people during Sadaam Hussein's tenure and sought to overturn it. Since the war didn't go as planned that's certainly been the most prominent reason put forth, but during the initial clamor it was at best a back-burner item. The war, however, like most wars, was most likely begun for a host of reasons, but this war was initiated prematurely, and that, now, is little disputed outside the defensive little cadre who launched it.

Again, I've done my best to accept the excuse of bad intelligence. As is well known Hussein was supposed to be harboring weapons of mass destruction while having some sort of interplay with Al-Qaeda. Neither was true, and the world knows that now. Whether the Bush administration knew it or not, of course, is unknown and will likely remain that way. What we as a nation do know - from Bush to Howard Dean to the lady at the checkout counter - is that we launched a war - bloody at best, catastrophic at worst - on bad intelligence, which means that if nothing else we fell far short of doing everything we could have done to avoid it, and that we subsequently rushed to war in a panic. Someone initiated that emotion, and if it didn't originate with Bush himself it certainly came from his cabinet.

Nations receive bad intelligence all the time. Incompetent agents can play a hand, as can other countries when governed by secret motives. In the case of Iraq we relied heavily on Chinese and Russian intelligence. Apparently we accepted it blindly rather than considering the many reasons those places might have for beguiling us into a costly, difficult, and unpopular war. In addition, a great deal of both our own and foreign intelligence said no such threats existed, and at very worst - as far as the public knows - any existing threats weren't imminent. In short, even under the worst case there was plenty of time for alternatives. These, however, weren't pursued. Instead we heard the urgent voices of doom exhorting both Congress and the public to act immediately if we didn't want to suffer unspeakable consequences. That the war began under the heel of this false panic has been largely forgotten now that it's over two years old and the Middle East has accelerated its resistance to autocracy, a lapse that's allowed the purveyors of that panic further maneuverability behind its shield.

Recently, the target has been Social Security, and the panic being played is national bankruptcy. Implication is everything in this technique. The White House won't directly say the nation will unravel in a generation if these specific reforms aren't passed at once, but tone and subtlety certainly imply that it will. Once again - here as in Iraq - the administration's motives may be pure. Social Security does, in fact, need tweaking. Very few voices outside Bush's cabinet, however, say there's anything remotely close to urgency or that any untended minor problems now will result in nothing short of an economic apocalypse. Unfortunately, the administration is famous for obstinacy and has a very precise reform agenda. Even its creators admit it will initially be very costly and have undetermined results in the future. These caveats are scarcely mentioned, though, as that would instigate both doubt and an ensuing debate for which there is plenty of time. Rather than subject this agenda, then, to compromise, a sense of hysteria needs to be injected in popular opinion, where - as with the Iraq War - the administration's policy will rush to approval relatively unsullied by the untidy but much preferred morphing of democracy.

It may work and it may not work, but so far people seem refreshingly resistant to the panic-mongering. Despite the cabinet's pleadings to the contrary, there's plenty of time to deliberate and everyone from senators to common citizens seems to understand that. Social Security, though, is one thing. Another war will be quite different. One problem with government of any kind is that it makes a valid and easy target for the populace to blame should things go badly, or even not as planned. Democracy is slightly different, as that validity is vitiated by the power the Constitution vests in both the citizenry at large and individuals in particular, a power that's often forgotten. We entrust the government to make the most reasonable choice available to them, though that obviously doesn't always happen. Even if Iraq turns out well, the mechanism of deliberation - democracy's most effective tool - withered beneath the heft of a drummed-up hysteria beat into America's people. We can blame the government for that, or we can work to ensure that we'll figure out for ourselves when we should and shouldn't panic. This country's government - no matter who's in office - can't move without at least half the people behind it. The next time, then, that the goat hooves start tapping across the country its people would do well to keep their composure a little longer and ask exactly what it is they're supposed to be afraid of this time. Poise is the greatest attribute in any situation, and a well-comported populace - democratically endowed to sway government decision-making if necessary - is this country's most vital component no matter how grave the problem. Bush and his people need to know that. Otherwise they'll just keep playing their pipes until the people tell them not to.

Chapter 8

Chalkboards, Swords, and Ploughshares

There's been a running battle over the last hundred years concerning religion's place in the classroom. Much of this, unfortunately, occurs on the periphery, over matters such as prayer or whether words like 'god' and 'Christmas' have any place in a public forum. This skirts the issue, lumping religion and theology as a single entity. Religious orthodoxies are only the frameworks we've developed with the immaterial material mined from human theology, and these structures, verifiable or no, have given our species much of the stability and cohesion necessary in an otherwise arbitrary, fugitive world. By putting the focus on religion - usually Christianity - educational leaders elide the spiritual aspects of our nature, and with them not only an intrinsic part to our whole but in theology arguably the best tool we have to foster critical abstract thought, a quality far superior to the current emphasis on standardized tests for building an intellectually agile culture. In exchanging this opportunity for the petty skirmishes now being fought, everyone from atheists to fundamental creationists deprives each generation - and therefore the country - of a more vibrant national theology. In turn, re-viving this debate would go far in granting America what participatory democracy needs most - a populace of critically robust, free-thinking individuals.

Everyone has a personal relationship to God. Whoever first contemplated divine possibility initiated theology, forcing every person since to grapple with their own definition of - and relation to - the ethereal. Subsequently matters have complicated. Across time and cultures theories have ramified from that first seed to great entanglements that individuals must negotiate. First they decide upon belief itself. If they believe, they either choose from hundreds of orthodoxies or leave the garden altogether to till a plot of their own. However it turns out for them one fact is certain - God cannot be avoided, and it's extraordinarily unhealthy to think it can be.

People as a whole possess an irrepressible spiritual instinct, an intuition reflective of our larger nature. At times it's instructive, inspiring, and cohesive, but can simultaneously be divisive, murderous, and hateful. America, by liberating the state from a specific creed, is built to extract theology's most salubrious qualities while mitigating if not outright dissolving its gravest dangers. Our religious fervor has always fluctuated across generational timelines, but it's never been the over-riding governance in any of our salient moments, high or low. Though it's played significant roles in everything from the Revolution to the Civil War to Civil Rights, America's secular concerns have always counterbalanced it. The two, in fact, have fortified one another quite effectively, making an odd but dynamic marriage that's supplied most of the inertia in building a sometimes great, sometimes wicked, but always powerful nation.

After nearly a century of public secular dominance, however, that pairing - alternating but balanced - is in danger of toppling, as the nation's spirituality never went away. In fact, it's now as powerful as ever, and it's effort to re-establish itself may go too far. George Bush, it turns out, might be the fulcrum wherein we're able to re-gain that stasis, resuming our need for spiritual inquiry while confining religion itself to the osmotic influence it's played in the past, an influence that for the most part has served us well. The trick will be restoring the balance without letting slip the destructive passion revolving deep within spirituality that can devastate like a split atom when released. Bush himself, ironically, isn't the hope so much as the prominence of his Christian faith is. Though I personally abhor the idea of a man openly entrusting world decisions to what he believes as a reciprocal dialogue with his own vision of God, I've come to realize this was probably inevitable.

Secular extremists may be the cause here. A natural recession in religious enthusiasm starting about the time of the Civil War was exacerbated by the scientific zealotry traced to natural selection theory. This wave lasted through about the nineteen seventies, an extended period in which a large share of the population saw in science a refracted messiah, a force many believed would unlock most if not all the universe's great secrets. Science has gone incalculably far in easing our lives during this time, but it's failed to make any theological gains other than to plague with doubt traditional creationist myths for all but the most obstinately faithful. Starting in the twenties, science began to dominate public education regarding the birth of the universe and life's creation. This combined with a slough of other social forces that by the sixties many had associated with religious repression, most notably sex. The country exploded, and organized religion - in terms of public life - was sent reeling.

What started as a backlash to heavy-handed Christian mores, however, went too far, making the seventies the most hedonistic decade in American history without the political compass of the sixties to validate it. This excess was unfortunate. Intermingled with the sex, drugs, and manifold political protests of the sixties was an enormous effort to entirely remove religion from public schools. It worked, but too well. Prayer was banished to the point that in recent years a kindergarten girl near Los Angeles was admonished for whispering grace before a meal. Each year - perhaps most vituperatively after the 2004 election - education boards, teachers, and parents battle over the use of Christmas and other religious symbolism in school observances. There's a worthy argument here, but it defeats itself when teachers are reprimanded for casually flipping a 'Merry Christmas' to someone in the hallway, as so often happens. Secularists - at least as defined by their desire to wipe religion from the public sphere - have over the last three decades exploited their momentum with the same arrogance as when religious zealots feel they have an advantage. This, for many reasons, was foolish, first among them numbers.

Americans are religious people. White, black, Asian, Hispanic, American Indian, East Indian - it doesn't matter. Nearly all of us identify with God in some way, whether through a church or not. For the most part even the cultural rebels of the sixties didn't lose their zest for divine contemplation, even as many of them strayed from the Christian fold. Buddhism, for instance, found a solid niche during this time, as did Islam among many black Americans. Others found their afflatus through nature. This vibrant quest for God - and the attendant comforts, inquiry, structure, and peace people find in the search - has not only maintained itself during the backlash but thrived, to the point that now that it's regained its footing those who oppose it are looking up at a larger, if not mightier, army than they. With a fervent Christian now in the White House this debate is bound to culminate, which, if done right, could instate both theology and historical religion to a level where they've never been in public education. Once there they'll do two things - cease the denial that religion has played an enormous role in all civilizations, and equally come to terms with the fact that spirituality is an integral part of human existence. Taught alongside empirical process and theory, kids will enhance the critical thinking skills that education was largely stationed to perform in the first place. Unfortunately the debate - mostly from intransigence on both sides - may not go right, retrogressing to a pattern of repetition where the religious advocates will go forward as uncompromising as their secular antagonists, resulting in a heavily theistic curriculum that will inevitably produce another cultural uprising. It's in the country's best interest to avoid that cycle.

Like most people, I don't remember much of what my teachers covered in high school. I do, though, specifically recall very little if any mention of religion, Christianity or otherwise. I can't say I gave that absence much thought at the time, but this in no way meant theology wasn't significant to me. Often this entailed what it does for the over-whelming majority of teenagers - an internecine introspection on the divine, everything from its existence to its form to its purpose. My parents made a conscious decision not to take their kids to church, feeling exposure to a single creed would invariably warp individual speculation. I'll be forever in debt to them for that decision. However, by the time I reached high school my own thoughts on the subject would've benefited greatly from different perspectives, just as somebody who has grown up Jewish, Jesuit, or Methodist needs those beliefs challenged. Whether it strengthens or shatters those holdings is irrelevant, for faith of any kind simply isn't authentic until it's tested intellectually. While there are plenty of places to find this debate beyond school, rarely do seventeen year olds find themselves all in one room with a topic as volatile as the existence or non-existence of God. Euclidean Law, dangling modifiers, and the reign of Julius Caesar are all necessary and worthy subjects, but there's not much room for a student to alter the course of conversation, and nothing stirs the mind - particularly at that age - like volatility among peers.

It's this very quality, however, that makes introducing theology and religion into public schools such a delicate matter. It's not so much the students. Kids would most likely throw their arms open to not only ideas that may differ radically from that of their parents, but to being in a conversation where what they say is no more wrong or right than the next person, including the teacher. Teachers themselves, though, would be mixed on the issue, as would parents, and it's here where the chemistry will likely keep the curriculum either entirely devoid of theological concerns or overly suffused with a specific dogma, which in the case of America means Christianity. This is the usual pattern when two parties are at loggerheads. Like armies perpetually hitting each other's right flank they constantly revolve around one another, alternating the high ground but never finding the stability to come to resolution. In the case of religion in the classroom, this unproductive dance results from two things - one, each side has its points and refuses to compromise, and two, each side fails to see that there in fact should not be two sides, but rather one debate with the aim of buttressing the critical powers of students while acknowledging that both secular and religious thought have contributed mightily to human accomplishment, both good and bad. This is so because human beings - individually and collectively - have both interests coursing through them at all times.

This preferred middle ground, however, will never be achieved unless each party understands the other, and in so doing comprehends the validity of certain concerns from both interests while relinquishing their own endmost positions. In the case of secularists, people against them could start with the term itself. It's very foolish to believe that 'secularist' indicates a non-spiritual person. In American political context the term is often taken as non-Christian, which for a fair number of people translates as atheist. Though a good number who vehemently oppose any form of theology in public schools refer to themselves as atheist, many more aren't. Some no doubt are Christian. These people - godly, atheist, agnostic - want anything related to spirituality banished from classrooms for many reasons, but they all stem from two roots - the separation of church and state and an extremely valid caution springing from even a cursory knowledge of religious history.

The separation of church and state is a tough one. Like most of the Constitution it seems half-written, a sort of a peek-a-boo mandate. This is difficult because so many see it as so simple. For those who want no mention of religion anywhere in the public sphere the phrase is taken literally. Others don't see it that way, and they have a point. The fragment itself isn't in the Constitution but from a letter of Thomas Jefferson's. The actual words, the first in the Bill of Rights, state that "Congress shall make no law respecting an establishment of religion, or prohibiting the free exercise thereof." That of course can be interpreted correctly as the separation of church and state. Difficulty arises, however, with any issue where human interpretation is possible. The words can also be correctly described as saying law only forbids the state from installing a specific religion as the national creed. From this angle it says nothing of preventing the free discussion of either singular dogmas or general theology in a public forum, and since there's no mention of schools this could reasonably assume public education as one of those forums. I personally agree with this interpretation, but with the petrified caveat that the favorable bias of a specified religion never be allowed the scarcest toe-hold, a feat that would take perpetual acrobatics. Fortunately, they're certainly achievable by inserting a detached religious history within any curriculum offering comparative religion and general theology.

Because secondary schools don't cover religion in any consequential detail, many people - even the highly inspired - never consider the range of spiritual emotions. These feelings are extant outside religion, of course, but when mixed with the momentum of divine certainty they become dangerous passions. Self-righteousness is among them, as are paranoia, rage, and fear. This ugly combination can incubate for generations beneath the gentler aspects of our nature, themselves often heightened by religion - compassion, discipline, communal respect, and love. It's only a matter of time, however, before a given social landscape releases the deadlier traits, and as is well-known a people united by the assurance of God's favor produce a febrile violence that can leave societies in shambles along with thousands of dead. History is too replete with examples to refute this, and students would need to be shown that they pervade all economic, political, and racial lines and that no major religion is exempt. Japan used Buddhist detachment to train kamikazes. The meteoric rise of Islam made an abattoir of Arabia and North Africa. If a tenth of the Torah is based on fact the early Jews shed seas of blood in God's name as well. And, since four out five Americans are Christian, it would certainly be useful to include details likely left out of Sunday services and current school curriculums alike.

America the nation was founded by northwest Europeans, at the time nearly all Christian. This fact is pointed out repeatedly by those favoring not only a religious influx in schools but one with a prominent Christian tint. In terms of history - which should be biased only in interpreting facts and not the facts themselves - these people are dead right. An American history course is scarcely half-told without the substantial role religion played - and continues to play - in its development. The Great Awakening, for instance, instilled the emphasis on individual primacy adopted by the generations authoring both independence and the Constitution. This fact is far too instrumental to be left out, but it's also one that can be accurately balanced by giving equal credence to both secular law and the Enlightenment as forces governing those same generations. Here students could study firsthand how porous the definitions 'secular' and 'religious' really are, permeating each other constantly in both the processes of people's lives and the decisions they make.

Caution, though, remains prudent. The great fear of those wishing to keep religion out of schools arises from the real threat that Christianity will assume supremacy and see classrooms become the nurseries of theocracy. This would obviously countermand the freedom of religion, but is an objection that not only few Americans oppose but also one that doesn't need explanation. There are other, more subtle reasons, however, to keep Christianity's influence on equal terms. One involves stagnation, the other boundless violence, but they both come from the same general fear of state religion.

Christian advocates rightly point out the binding communal powers that Puritanical Christianity afforded Massachusetts' first generation, which secured America's cultural seeds. Side by side, though, lie other crucial facts rarely mentioned. Though fleeing its religious persecution, the Puritans inevitably brought with them their English culture, which through the Anglican Church included a state religion. State religions produce three things - mindless obeisance, distracting tedium, and rampant bloodshed. Most cultures under such rule experience all three in cyclical fashion, while an energetic national theology tends to thrive in places where free worship reigns. Because of their common roots and Christian majorities, Europe as a whole and England specifically would be the most relevant examples when comparing the fate of imposed religion against that of free choice.

Puritanism was an offshoot of the Protestant Reformation, which in its successful effort to divorce individual choice from the Roman Church - or central power - was another great push on American philosophy. The Church gained ascendancy in Europe by effective proselytizing, but also by wide-spread other means including warfare and deceit. Charlemagne was particularly brutal, and the chief reason early America's polytheistic European ancestors were Christianized. Frustrated by Saxon obstinacy, the Frankish king cut off forty-five hundred heads in a single day to persuade those remaining. The use of *The Heliond*, as well, a Saxon Gospel translation, converted others. Knowing some tribal factions would never revere a pacifist, Jesus in this version was a mighty warrior who gashed Judas with a broadsword rather than kissing him. Though these incidents may now seem irrelevant they're not, as people should know both the good and bad in how their chosen religion came down to them.

Early Christianity's other dark moments are well known and widely acknowledged. The Inquisition earns the greatest infamy, as do indulgences and other means of exploitation. It was these that largely led to Martin Luther and the Reformation, where for a century and a half Europe learned the grimmest aspects that human religion can arouse. From the *Wildwuchs* in Germany to St. Bartholomew's Day in France to the alternating burnt Protestants and Catholics in England through to the decades' long carnage of the Thirty Year's War, Europe literally roiled in blood and fire. With nearly everyone believing the Last Days were imminent, Catholics and Protestants killed each other and themselves in horrific numbers. Americans still shudder at the 1692 Salem witch spate that killed nineteen people, but in a century's time fifty thousand others suffered the same fate across Europe. By the time Europe's bloody religious quarrels were subsiding into the Enlightenment, America's first communities were taking root, and if they didn't bring the Anglican Church with them, it didn't take them long to revive the notion of a state faith, which may well have presented the same galling fractures had such rigidity been allowed to form. Thankfully that never happened.

In Massachusetts the Puritan's phased into Congregationalists, and it was this austere brand of Christianity they wished to mandate. Struggling to do so, they failed. Roger Williams, following the lead of Anne Hutchinson, broke ranks, establishing Rhode Island where free worship was permanently rooted in the American psyche. Though Williams was a Calvinist and believed everyone who wasn't - along with many who were - would burn in hell, he didn't feel it was the right of men to initiate those sufferings on earth. "All men may walk as their consciences persuade them," he declared, "every one in the name of his God." This was the beginning of America's split between secular and church law, and through this dictum it would grant its citizens not only individual choice but also emancipate theology - potentially one of a culture's great gifts to the world - from the slow death of autocratic thought. In terms of Europe, the stagnation of Catholic inquiry led to corruption, decay, and the abuse of poorly educated populaces. That formula produces violent overturn every time and it came in this case with the Reformation. England's own establishment of a state church produced similar bloodshed. Though other political factors have con-tributed, mandated Islam in many Middle Eastern cultures is currently showing similar unrest. The suppression of theological inquiry, then, not only severely restricts a basic tenet of humanity - that of spiritual pursuit - but for the very reason that same tenet is so elusive its denial removes one of the great topics of human debate. In the meantime these restrictions foster a lethargy in populations that over generations tends to rapid and violent punctuation rather than a more vibrant but stable consistency.

This is what America got right. However, by opening schools up to both theology and religious history, exposing younger people to such discourse could improve it that much more. Ironically, those likely to prevent this overturn - people fearful of allowing religion in - are the ones who would be pleasantly surprised, and the ones who champion the change the people likely to be unexpectedly upset. This, of course, assumes that Christianity is kept level with everything else. It must be remembered that were Christianity installed in public schools as the dominant dogma, its many factions would inevitably vie for their own dictatorial supremacy, producing irreconcilable quarrels and probable violence. As such, religious teachings must be kept egalitarian. Were that achieved, suddenly Baptists and Mormons, Presbyterians and Seventh Day Adventists, Muslims and Pentecostals, Jews and Catholics, atheists and agnostics, would all be in the same room, hearing largely for the first time open opinions both subtley and vastly different from those of their upbringing. The history of their religions, as well, might be exposed in ways they hadn't been before. Evolution would be taught alongside various creation myths, and kids could debate and ultimately decide for themselves how they think the universe came to be, or whether or not it's governed, and, if governed, how. Many individual faiths would be shaken in this way, which would upset religion-oriented parents while pleasing those of more unorthodox beliefs. Many kids' faiths would also solidify. Regardless, the students would gain the most here. Cerebral volatility produces creative thought, and creative thought produces a more upright individual. At a time in their lives when they're likely to be the most privately inquisitive, kids will be thrust into discussing the existence or non-existence of God, the character and form of such a being, and it's presence or absence in their lives. This will be translated into humanity as a whole, where they'll be exposed to the spiritual and secular drives that move both individuals and civilizations to do what they do. Through all this they'll have a far greater chance of becoming challenging thinkers, and generations of such people will not only put forth a more radiant theology, but on the whole become a multi-dimensional, mentally dexterous nation.

Chapter 9

The Most Pleasing Time

The proposed 2005 budget showed at least one promising sign, as among the many domestic cuts is a long-needed move to reduce farm subsidies. What the Bush administration's motives are here I don't know, but they're probably little more than an effort to reduce the deficit. Though the national debt is indeed a problem, however, cutting farm subsidies could have benefits stretching far beyond the process of budget-mending. For one the United States has been an early and long-standing proponent of globalization, and though we've advocated and for the most part held our own on international no-tariff policies, we've been rightly labeled hypocrites when it comes to propping up farmers. The situation, though, is tricky. Firstly, it would be political suicide for any office-holder to immediately stop all funding. Secondly, and of far greater import, it would likely be ruinous to both the nation's agriculture as well as the international food supply. Along with farm technology and abundant arable land the subsidizing installed during the Depression allowed American agriculture to thrive, and this explosion owes a great deal to the fact that we supply much of the world's staple food. To suddenly implode this system would produce seismic swells from Iowa to Europe to Africa to China. The shift needs to be slow, then, but steady, and the fallout could positively address many frictions now grating in America - from the potentially catastrophic to the simply irritable. It would involve a restructuring of American farm culture, and encompass the best of two worlds: while satisfying some fundamental tenets of the country's ideology it would have the critical benefit of doing so based on economic and diplomatic principles rather than pure nostalgia.

America's roots in the family farm have been mythologized for decades now, and the loss of this base much lamented for some time. Though it's particularly acute during political campaigns, the dwindling remnants of America's yeoman families provide a melancholic backbeat to a country otherwise giddy for modernity. Many, many people - from the independent farmers themselves to others in places as remote as Manhattan and Houston - mourn the steady way in which industrial agriculture digests smaller-scale farms every year. Prior to globalization, however, this sentiment was more akin to the loss of childhood than anything else - a regrettable transition from a simple past but one endowed with all the efficiencies and acumen of maturity. In short, conglomerates may be intrusive and faceless but they yield bounties well beyond the collective dreams of the country's family farming ancestry. Problems, though, remain ample. That bounty has come with a heavy environmental price, and one that may undo us not many generations from now. Combined, then, with the political quicksand of continued subsidies under globalization and a genuine yearning of many Americans to return to the country, this broad confluence could well make the most pleasing time to re-establish the family farm.

Subsidies themselves wouldn't have to stop, but just need re-aligning from the current format of favoring trusts. Graced with these spoils the industrial farms have in the last seventy years inhaled the bulk of productive land. For decades that seemed to serve the country well, producing a fantastic surplus that not only enriched our export potential but provided quite a bargaining chip in tight diplomatic situations, such as the prolonged wrangling of the Cold War or the more recent squabbles with North Korea. Now, though, with rising environmental concerns colliding with a restructured global economy, agriculture might want to reverse its established trend of consolidation and move once again toward the smaller, more numerous units of the past. Shifting government help from the large to the small, then, would break these conglomerates up, redistributing land in far smaller parcels to any family willing to farm it. In many ways it would be a far less hectic version of the 1862 Homestead Act, and - though for different reasons - could have the same success. While there would certainly be an adjustment period, its turbulence could be significantly mitigated by an incremental rather than a sudden shift. In the meantime American agriculture could perform four turn-arounds in as many fields - international integrity, environmental healing, market strategy, and further options in the slight but noticeable trend of moving from city to country. These fields additionally share an agreeable plot of common ground, and this overlap buttresses even further the case for small-unit farming.

By itself international integrity sanctions a complete gutting of the farm subsidy program. Along with China and perhaps India, no one country has bent the world's will more toward globalization than America. While this relatively sudden shift has caused abundant disparity world-wide - a disparity protectionist economies discourage - enough inertia is behind it that by now it will have to run its course. It may even work, and the day will come when free trade provides the greatest benefit for the greatest amount of people, a utilitarian's dream. Free, though, means just that - free. As a driving influence behind free trade, America can't make exceptions anywhere, especially in farm subsidies, as much of the developing world suffers greatly under these props. Africa, for instance, needs a lot of help in a lot of places. By cutting American cotton subsidies - by adhering to principles of free trade in other words - Africans could make some gains in cotton exports. The same could be said for wheat and rice, where regions such as eastern Europe and southeast Asia would respectively have the comparative advantage. America and Americans steep themselves in enough hypocrisy culturally, almost too much to enumerate. Abroad, though, we should do our best to present one face to the world, particularly with such a seemingly simple framework as free trade. Foreign diplomacy sometimes requires great measures of duplicity and counter-duplicity and our ability to maneuver in these more delicate situations would be far more liberated if we removed the glaring paradox of touting globalization while not practicing it ourselves.

Cutting agri-business subsidies, of course, would drive many large-scale farms under, which on it's face is bad business. Much greater goods, though, lie underneath, and all of them related. Though American farm output continues to swell, it's been known for sometime that the excessive abuse has strained our cultivated land to dangerous lengths. The Dust Bowl of the Depression was certainly indicative of the problems rapacious tilling presents, and the current dead zone fanning out from the Mississippi Delta is a palpable testament to the lethal effects aggressive fertilization has upon waterways and fisheries. No one wants these problems, if for no other reason than they threaten or outright curb other economic opportunities such as future agriculture or commercial fishing. While practices such as no-till farming, grass-feeding cattle, and organic farming are taking root in order to counter these difficulties, the pace needs to be greatly accelerated. Reducing both farm size and the amount of land farmed would help immensely, and fortunately recent market trends seem to support these shifts.

As consumers become more educated to the dangers pesticides and anti-biotics pose both to the land on which they're used and the human body itself, the organic farming industry has enjoyed exponential growth for some time now. Like any new trend or product, of course, this upward mobility has and will slow as it reaches various stages of fulfilled potential. The industry itself, however, has surpassed its initial niche role and is set for long-term growth, particularly as competition, market expansion, and efficiency work to lower prices. Organic farms tend to be much smaller than industrial operations, and combined with the fact that they have less impact on the land their increased capacity would go far in convalescing the hurt the American soil has taken in the last couple of centuries. In addition, though it's currently much more incipient than the organic fruit and vegetable trend, there's been some initial market movement toward grass-fed beef. Cattle are meant to graze, or eat grass. For decades now beef cows have been fattened just prior to slaughter by largely immobilizing herds while feeding them corn. This practice leads to fat-heavy beef as well as the necessity of pumping animals full of anti-biotics to counter the ill effects of feeding them what they weren't intended to eat. About forty-percent of the nation's grain crop goes to feed livestock. By shifting back to the healthier practice of grazing cattle that number could be reduced dramatically, freeing up land for other purposes, such as letting it go fallow before farming it again in smarter ways. Demand, of course, will dictate whether or not such transitions occur, but early indicators support the trend toward grass-fed cattle. By shifting from subsidies for enormous operations that grain-feed livestock, then, to offering either tax-relief or tax-exemption to smaller operations that employ healthier practices, America would greatly encourage an already rising market trend while simultaneously satisfying its international obligations regarding free trade. The same could be said of cutting subsidies to large-scale farms that rely on pesticides and anti-biotics for vegetable production while giving tax breaks to organic entrepreneurs. If the larger, chemical-driven farms survive, they'll do so through market support rather than government stilts, leveling the global economy as free trade is meant to level it.

One more socially-driven factor makes the move from large to small farms both an attractive and natural one at this time. In a reverse from a centuries old trend dating back to Europe people are now moving out of the city and into the country. Technology has largely enabled small businesses to operate in rural areas where before it was impossible. Liberated in this way many former urban and suburban dwellers are happily migrating either to the country itself or a new sphere called the ex-urbs, the border between suburb and farm country, and while many of these recent migrants make their living in businesses such as finance, marketing, or technological consultation, they also move to rural settings because they enjoy the rural life. At least a few, I'm sure, wouldn't mind trying their hand at small farm operations, especially if enticed by tax breaks. In addition, others who want to move to the country but don't perform information-age type work that allows them to do so - such as factory workers, mechanics, or construction people - would certainly consider the change if small-scale farming was a viable option. Should the government cease subsidizing the conglomerates in favor of tax relief to smaller, family-sized units, then many of the big operations would go bankrupt, freeing up enormous tracts of good farm land. Many rural states, mostly in the mid-West, are already actively recruiting people to re-juvenate their dwindling and increasingly crime-ridden populations. As in 1862, these areas would once again have the great lure of land and the opportunity to farm it to attract people to their communities. Whatever acreage didn't get farmed could go to other uses, such as letting it go wild again to provide more opportunities for hunting and other outdoor recreation, a bonus not many Americans would oppose. A great many people, then, want to move to the country. Once there at least a percentage would want to actively engage in the rural economy.

Coincident with this social phenomenon, a more educated consumer base - weary of toxic albeit hugely productive farming practices - have established a solid market for organic meat and produce, products that favor small-unit farming. Additionally, beyond America's borders, the United States has the unavoidable obligation of sticking to the principles of free trade that this country has pushed since that idea's conception. First and foremost this means the removal of federal farm subsidies, however gradual that process needs to be. All these factors have combined to form a perfectly natural event, one that favors a return to the family farm. It's a trend that's always been freighted with sentiment within the American populace, but one that now rests firmly on diplomatic and economic principles as well.

Chapter 10

Boomsticks

Shotguns are endemic to my life. I've hunted with my father every autumn since I was twelve, pursuing ruffed grouse in northeastern Pennsylvania. No matter where either of us are living we've managed to meet at his cabin there each Thanksgiving week, to trap muskrats and mink and hunt birds in the same derelict orchards and broken hemlock stands we've known for decades. For years, as well, we hunted up and down the Housatonic Valley in northwestern Connecticut and spent a couple falls chasing both grouse and woodcock in central Vermont when I lived there. I've been in Alaska a few years now and he's come up for a week each October. The land is wet and expansive and we spend the daylight stalking ducks and geese along the tidal flats and inland swamps. These experiences are so entwined with my larger memory that I'd be half hollow without them, but it goes well beyond that. Both my father and I anticipate these gatherings the way the devout yearn for ritual. There's a solemnity in the wait, a sobriety, but also the passionate attachment of tradition. So much of what we know of each other and the world comes through hunting that we'd be different, lesser people without that perspective.

It never occurred to me as a kid, therefore, that people opposed gun ownership or that they'd even think to do so. Before I could hunt I remember my father heading out, putting the long, two-barreled gun in the trunk of his car. I suppose I was aware of warfare and the danger of firearms, but it seemed remote then, even other-worldly. When I was able to go with him, to handle a gun, I realized the piece itself had nothing to do with it, but what it allowed you to perform. It was a tool, a mechanism to interact with the natural world, the way a fiddle or guitar allows someone to make and take part in music - the feel of the instrument in your hand only carries meaning for the deeper experience it permits. After hunting for a couple years, getting to know the woods, seeing how well my father moved through a forest, learning where grouse are and why, I came to appreciate the gun in my hands through the multi-layered depth it granted. I was, however, learning other things at the time, and among them was that American people both desired and used guns for different purposes than my own, and that a great many others opposed firearms on all grounds. This was news, but by now I've come to see the issue as all people do, as an individual with both particular interests and the only cognizant filter I know of, my own perceptions. Though I've formed a definitive opinion on the subject, I've reached it by several routes, and along the way realized that as with all charged issues both sides have their points.

For years I really only had an attachment to guns through hunting. The truth is, neither my father nor I have much interest in guns, at least technically or historically the way many people do. We each own a duck gun and a grouse gun, which means a twelve and twenty gauge shotgun respectively. They're oiled, cleaned, and well cared for, but when other people start talking in technical terms neither of us stays in the conversation long. We like them for what they do for us, not for how they're made. Since I've moved to Alaska I've purchased a rifle and have become familiar with several others, but again I admire them only for their utility. Some of this may be cultural. Growing up in southwestern Connecticut - the bedroom of New York City - I didn't know many gun owners. A few friends' fathers had a range pistol, several others hunted deer, and there was the occasional historical piece, but guns certainly weren't in the community's grain. As such, and living under the tent of the New York nightly news, I had great exposure to the bleaker side of the second amendment, which certainly offered resistance to my earlier, more favorable opinions on firearms.

As in all tight debates there are certain glaring facts with which each side must contend. One of them, touted with authority by gun opponents, is that every year an awful lot of Americans shoot each other. Certain statistics become specifically moot when they reach a given point. While it's critical to follow annual trends to the number, when gunshot victims go into the many thousands words like 'a lot' and 'a bunch' serve better than an actual number in general argument, simply meaning 'too many'. My first impressions of this sustained epidemic came straight out of its heart. I've heard dozens of people claim with macabre pride that their mid-sized city has the highest per capita murder rate, and maybe one them is right. For sheer numbers, though, it's tough to beat New York. Back in the days of three channel television there wasn't much choice at news hour, and if you were watching New York TV you were watching the daily death toll. It seemed two or three people were shot there every day, sometimes more. Through this I first understood the grievances people had with guns, and after a while it's tough not to see those points as authentic. The gun rights squad, of course, has to answer for this. It's an ugly fact that firearms are often used for ill purposes, and it's not easy to tell someone whose lost a friend or family member to a shooting that all Americans should have the right to carry any gun at any time. This argument can and has been made, but it must be done by means other than draping yourself in a flag and stammering out the half-truth that the Constitution gives you that right. All too often, though, that's the knee-jerk response, and since it's these laws that govern our jurisprudence, the second amendment itself should be looked at first.

In its own way the right to bear arms is Constitutionally trickier than other sticking points plaguing the document. Ironically the friction is due to direct wording. The whole law says this: "A well regulated Militia, being necessary to the security of a free State, the right of the people to keep and bear Arms, shall not be infringed." There's not much equivocal in that. Roe vs. Wade, on the other hand, is Constitutionally upheld even though you'd only find the phrase "abortion rights" if you disassembled the doctrine itself and played Scrabble. "Separation of church and state" is another one. Though the first amendment comes somewhat close, it never - as staunch secularists advocate - specifically precludes any talk of God or religion in a public forum. Gun rights, then, should be a no-brainer - ". . . the right of the people to keep and bear arms . . .". There's a peep-hole of ambiguity when the words 'militia' and 'people' are linked, for it can and has been argued that only citizens actively engaged in militia training can bear arms, but that's a stretch. The Constitution itself, afterall, opens with 'We the People . . .', indicating a nation first comprised of individuals liberated to regulate themselves. It's not the wording, then, that causes the trouble, but the document's own nature coupled with the viscous properties of cultural paradigm.

The Constitution was never meant to be rigid. It's authors, though maddeningly vague at crucial points, weren't stupid. They knew their history, and in knowing history they knew permanent law led to impermanent states. Cultures are affected by many things over time - technology, shifting mores, external threat, internal faction, and many others - and a nation's laws must be as flexible as the world is fluid. This is the Constitution's guiding genius. Guns have changed, and people who own them most likely have - if nothing else - a much more confident approach in their use of them than they did in 1787. In short, firearms are more effective and people's zeal for them has shifted accordingly, often to perilous extremes. This is where unthinking gun proponents look foolish. They've heard this argument before, and rather than responding with reason they simply roll their eyes and point to the second amendment. Facts are facts, they'll say, and the fact is private gun ownership is Constitutionally protected. Given other facts, though, this is questionable.

In defending British soldiers against the Boston Massacre John Adams made himself famous by saying "Facts are stubborn things." He may have added they're reactive things as well, bonding on to other facts to form new compounds with characters entirely different than the original. The Constitution says the people have a right to bear arms. That's a fact. It's also a fact that guns were nearly more trouble than they were worth when that was written. Rifles were long, heavy, and highly inaccurate. Their effective range wasn't much different than an arrow, and if you shot once it would be some time before you could shoot again. Pistols weren't any better. The abysmal records of duelists standing paces apart and missing each other pays testament to that. In addition, no matter what piece you carried, any dampness in the powder, any mistake as you frantically re-loaded, any quirk of any kind for any reason, and you may as well have hurled the gun rather than fired it. A madman in eighteenth century Philadelphia could walk into a pub, kill one man with one round then wait to be clubbed to death. The same man today can buy a Glock at Wal-Mart, wait five days to pick it up, then leave as many dead as fast as he can shoot and change clips. Automatic rifles, of course, compound the difficulty, as does sniper weaponry, as the DC shooter proved with solemn clarity.

The Revolutionary period itself, of course, must be considered as well. The British were defeated in large part because people owned and were proficient with guns before the war. Additionally, as the new nation found it's uneasy footing no one knew whether France or Britain or Spain would be the next threat, they only knew that threat was plausible. Internal faction presented other problems. We talk of division today, but uprisings like Shay's Rebellion and the Whiskey Rebellion were real events carried out by men with guns. Lastly, as uncomfortable as many Americans - white Americans to be specific - are with this thought today, the truth is Indians were a cause for fright in the late eighteenth century. Whether or not we believe now that Natives were justified in their attacks was irrelevant to people living with those attacks. Scalpings, torture, and massacres were facts then, and elements such as religion, race, cultural difference, and outright land thirst prevented most in the burgeoning country from seeing Indians as anything but a threat to be confronted. We see it differently now, we didn't then. We've shifted.

Today, then, whether cultural circumstance or technological advancement is more responsible I don't know, but people's attitudes towards guns have changed. We've polarized from what today we'd undoubtedly view as a more centrist position in the Constitutional era. Gun advocates, backed by enormous political clout, have crowded around both the second amendment and tradition with defiant tenacity. Their opponents have done all they can do in the face of long-standing legislation and a cultural heritage steeped in gun use. With the strength of great truths behind them, they've pointed to changes in gun technology and the cultural sensibilities that have attended them, along with the vanished menaces of Indians, the British, and Daniel Shay, all of whose modern versions can be handled by our substantial military and police forces. The second amendment itself is still relevant, then, as are the traditions that have shaped a great portion of our country, from individuals to families to whole regions. But the modern facts are relevant, too, such as appalling gun death rates, AK-47's, and the significant part of Americans who are aloof of the gun culture largely because of these changes. These opposing sides are today's facts, and it's from them - more than wording - that each individual must negotiate the second amendment.

Though it's taken me some time to get there I'm all for guns. I don't much identify with the boisterous crowd who insist on pointing out every detail of each piece in their considerable collection, including what it can and can't do to a human being. However, with some legislative quibbling aside, we'd probably agree with each other on polling day. A lot of people want no restrictions or regulation on any firearm for any reason at any time. I disagree on some points, but for the most part we're in accord. How anybody, for instance, could be against a five-day waiting period is beyond me. It simply removes a great deal of danger in the hours following a great trauma, such as eye-witnessed adultery. Background checks at gun shows are another one, particularly in the era of terror tactics both homegrown and foreign-born. For this same reason I wouldn't oppose any measure mandating gun registration for a year or more. The world's changed, and we ought to change with it. I'll never, though, agree to much more beyond these measures, though earlier in life I wouldn't have said that.

My support of nearly unmitigated gun rights comes down to two points - hunting and the benefits of an armed populace, which for me outstrip its several downsides. For years, though, hunting was the only portion of the debate that carried personal currency. Fortunately, it's also the most benign issue on the docket. Apart from those who oppose it on animal rights grounds, hunting is not generally considered the chief pathogen of gun ownership, and even anti-hunters tend to separate the second amendment from their ruling passion - animal cruelty. Many who want the second amendment either over-turned or greatly compromised would most likely give room to ownership of shotguns and deer rifles. This would obviously create a legislative quagmire, but a significant percentage of gun opponents I'm sure would willfully exchange hunting rights in the countryside for automatic rifles and handguns in the city. There's reasons for this.

Since civilization began there's been a huge rift between urban and rural culture. America is no different, and firearms are in the middle of that rift. It's no wonder then why the majority of both gun and hunting opponents come from the cities and the communities closest to them. Hunting, though, is far more complicated than many people are willing to believe, particularly those in congested communities whose families are entirely removed from it. Both urban and suburban cultures have been psychologically divested of the natural world, along with any concept that human beings still belong to those cycles. It's become cliche to say that people in these environments don't even think where their food comes from, but it bears repeating, since the separation of humanity and nature has occurred only in their minds. Though even in the country most of what people eat comes from far away places, they understand the connections between human sustenance and nature. Hunting, like gardening, allows people to dissolve that connection, to become part of the cycle rather than a mere beneficiary. As such, those outside the circle simply can't comprehend the stir that moves people to hunt each fall, and when that emotion - nearly unreachable by language - is enmeshed with family tradition it becomes an irrepressible rite, one that people unequivocally won't give up. While hunting itself hasn't suffered much beyond wise regulation based on sustainability, trapping may be an omen toward a highly uneasy divide between city and country in this nation. Many states, including ostensibly conservative places like Colorado and Arizona, have banned trapping. Rather than by county, the votes were statewide. Rural areas, where people trap, voted overwhelmingly in favor of the endeavor, whereas the cities and suburbs trounced it. When the numbers were tallied it wasn't even close. Scarcely anyone in the nation even hears of trapping, but plenty of people know about hunting, and should this same vote be applied to it - whether through an anti-gun measure or animal cruelty - I believe those ulterior to the activity will find just how rigid people can be when faced with losing their inmost tradition.

Many non-hunters and non-gun owners, however, understand this, and yet the gun issue persists. Here the divergence swings the other way, where people in the country need to stand in the shoes of those who live with gun violence on an elevated basis - the city dwellers. This is a tough one. I personally believe murder numbers go up in cities primarily because of congestion. Though there's an undeniable positive energy and fertile confluence of thought in cities, the crowding has a protruding downside. Open space not only quells human temper, it diffuses its general build-up. Hemmed in, constantly in contact with one another, people in cities accrue agitation at higher rates than those in the country; it pens up quicker and releases more often. Add firearms to that mix and there's going to be problems. Other factors such as poverty and concentrated markets for illicit entrepreneurship like drug trafficking compound the matter. Cities have always been more dangerous places than the country, and guns make them more so. This point must be conceded. For someone like me, who champions gun rights, it presents difficulty. I don't live in Atlanta, Chicago, or Los Angeles. As a trapper, I complain that statewide votes for certain matters would be more representative if conducted by county. Maybe city residents feel the same. I'd have little to say to someone in the Bronx, for instance, if they wanted to vote guns out only in that borough, the place where they live. I have, though, in the past few years come to see another side of gun support that I'd at least tout to them before they voted.

As an adult my first impression of political atmosphere was the Clinton years. Being fairly liberal in many ways I enjoyed that period immensely in terms of the country's political tilt. This included policy shifts such as greater stewardship measures, Clinton's openness about race and past foreign policy abuses, and an overall decent rapport with other nations. I'm also conservative in some ways, particularly fiscally, and Clinton shared that aim as well. My contentment, though, went far beyond fiscal awareness and policy debates. It came down to personal space. As egotistic as Clinton can be he never seemed to have much interest in foisting himself into people's lives. Though he attended church and claimed deep devotion, he was mostly private in his religion. He supported abortion rights but rarely if ever moralized why. He raised taxes but did so at a time when it needed doing, then took the money and quietly when about putting the country back on a financial keel. In short, I never felt crowded by him, and in fact half the time was scarcely aware he was even there. Louis Brandeis said the

Constitution essentially gives citizens the right to be left alone. Clinton seemed to agree with him.

I did, though, know full well others had their own opinions on the matter. All through those years I worked or was otherwise associated with at least a dozen people who hated Clinton, in particular for the Branch Davidian fiasco. They thought the incident both a gross abuse of government intrusion and a fine example of why citizens should have unrestricted gun rights. This set me back. I was young, and never really considered the possibility that the government would ever force its way into people's privacy. Besides, I thought the Davidians were dangerous people and still do. At the time, whenever someone stirred themselves up over the importance of private gun ownership to protect the general populace from government aggression I dismissed it as fringe-speak. Gradually, though, I've changed. First it was academic. I came to understand that the second amendment was in great part written with defense against rampant government in mind. I admire both historical precedent and the Constitution's authors in general and so quietly took that to heart. Still, having never felt any kind of threat myself, I remained wary of that particular aspect of the gun debate - it wasn't personal yet. Many times you simply can't field another's argument until you've stood where they stand. Clinton's policies, probably because I agreed with most of them, never offended me. Never once during those eight years did I feel or even think to feel that the government threatened my privacy, and I mostly scoffed at people who did. George W. Bush, however, has made me see things otherwise.

It comes down to personal make-up. As individuals we favor certain of a president's beliefs where other people see dire threats. In the nineties it never occurred to me that Clinton's private ambivalence toward abortion while publicly supporting it offended many people. His tax hikes to balance the budget I saw as responsible, not - as I now realize many people do - as an invasion of private income. That he's a committed Baptist who didn't publicly expound either the virtues of Christianity or the need to follow its creed simply seemed concordant with both American doctrine and culture. Others, as I now know, were enraged by these traits. With the successive elections of Bush, then, my eight years of innocence under Clinton died abruptly, and if I agree with nothing else with those who deeply admire the current president, we at least likely share the belief that the greatest check on government intrusion is a freely armed populace.

It's not the Patriot Act. Like most people I barely know what it says, and any excesses at least have the rationale of 9/11 to excuse if not sanction them. Besides, some of that bill's most absurd measures have recently been excised. Some of my change-of-heart, though, is policy. It took thirty years but by 2000 an environmental ethic first legislated by Richard Nixon had finally begun to bear some fruit. Bush has crippled that effort. While some see these as pro-business measures, I see them as acute violations of international health. Most of my grievances, however, rather than legislative, come from presidential intangibles, such as tone, presence, and implied morality. George Bush is unquestionably arrogant, but this in itself isn't an offense so much as what it leads him to. He's everywhere. After the Trade Towers fell I understood this, but in the years since I can't turn on a radio or television, pick up a newspaper, or log onto the internet without seeing Bush all over it, always in efforts to sell himself and his positions. I'm a firm believer in strong government but now that it's a daily interface in my life I've largely come to resent it. Bush's public ubiquity, too, has trickled down, where even a Supreme Court figure like Antonin Scalia muscles his way into the media from time to time.

Based on Bush's re-election I suppose many Americans enjoy this assertiveness, perhaps simply because they sanction his policies. Bush's constant media presence, too, as well as that of many of his GOP followers, is freighted with flagrant Christian overtones, and where this may please a slight majority of Americans, it riles me to no end. I don't need government officials implying either what form of God should be worshipped nor what constitutes morality. I'll figure that out for myself. Combined with Bush's popularity among Christian extremists and an unconcealed love for the military this has become a threat for me personally, if not yet grave then certainly one to be noted. From this angle I've seen the attraction of the second amendment in new terms. If staunch social conservatives support gun rights for fear of liberals forcing their way into their homes to take their guns, ban their bibles, and encourage their daughters to have abortions, then I've come to champion the same rights in case Rick Santorum and John Ashcroft show up at my doorstep with a bowl of Crisco and a vat of Holy Water

- at least I can rip off a couple rounds before their goons take me out. If the reasons are different, the sentiment's the same - guns are an effective stay against personal disruption.

Currently I favor the Democratic Party, as for the most part my views are in accord with its. As such, I certainly hope its elected officials allow gun rights to slide off the table. Mostly this is personal. As a hunter I couldn't think to separate myself from the experiences, ritual, and insights hunting affords, and recently I've been converted to an armed citizenry's effectiveness against wayward government. Should the party make it clear that the second amendment will live on unmolested - not because it was written that way but because it's still relevant despite the modern drawbacks - then it will open itself up to a great many voters. Hunting ties people to landscapes, nature, their families, and deep-seated traditions all over the country. It binds individuals, relatives, townships, and entire regions to form an inextricable, complex part of our culture. People know this, and many will vote against any candidate who even hints that this rite may be threatened. Americans, too, are notoriously suspicious of government, and I personally know many otherwise liberal people who heartily sanction gun rights as a protective measure against it. There's far too much at stake, then, for guns to weaken progressive thought, and the support against them simply isn't there.

My work in Alaska monitoring salmon runs puts me in frequent contact with brown bears. Everyone on the job carries a rifle. A recreational angler - who'd just had a bear false-charge him at close quarters then rear up on its legs before retreating - once asked me and a colleague what we'd do in that situation. My friend spoke first. "That's when you show him your boomstick," he said. Being from the northeast I probably lack the drama to ever say something like "from my cold, dead hands," but what we lack in dramatics we make up for in sarcasm. I can, then, say 'boomstick', and it's my fervent hope that the Democratic Party, with so much else to offer once it regains its feet, embraces the fact that boomsticks are here to stay.

Chapter 11

Europe

Something awful is going to happen in Europe soon. Though the Balkans recently put themselves through an ugly, low-grade war, the northwest has been quiet for six decades now, an unmatched record since anybody's kept track. It won't last. World War II - and in particular the Holocaust - changed the continent, an inevitability considering the horror. In the war's wake - and faced with a usurped Marxist ideology to the east - France, West Germany, and England, as well as the smaller countries, took a breather, re-organizing their definitions of wealth and power toward the general welfare while pushing away from the religious, social, and political ideology that had caused such a gruesome past. In the process they seem to have succeeded at least somewhat in creating highly tolerant societies capable of distributing wealth in such a way as to form a dignified quietude in the populace, replacing the explosive passions that've tortured the continent for a thousand years. Their pasts, though, by two different routes, will link to overturn that peace.

Fire needs three things - fuel, spark, and oxygen. In Europe's case their colonial past combined with their modern tolerance will provide the fuel. Islamic extremists will supply the spark, and the continent's flash temper - dormant now for sixty years - will feed the flame. Though Britain ended up doing it best, most European nations at least dabbled

in imperialism. This gave them great wealth, which allowed for tremendous innovation and cultural achievement. It also produced centuries of avarice, warfare, abuse of weaker peoples, and a mixed legacy
- always the result when foreign peoples clash, one dominating the
other. In modern terms the legacy of dissolved empires has produced
mixed results as well. Guilt and a genuinely tolerant atmosphere following World War II have combined to open Europe to the migrants
of former colonies. These more idealistic reasons have coupled in recent
years with the practicalities of an aging Continental population and
the growing disdain of wealthy countries to perform low-wage labor.
If many Europeans, then, look upon these newcomers with everything
from suspicion to outright loathing, they've let them in for the same
reason the United States always receives immigrants - to do work. In
the meantime they've done their best to accommodate these arrivals,
and while it's worked for a while it won't for long.

Religion, obviously, has a lot to do with it. Europe's solidly Christian
in name, but its fervor has waned to the point that agnostics now dominate. If any place on earth understands the havoc of fanatical religious
beliefs it's Europe. Today's lingering trouble in Northern Ireland is a
snowball fight compared to what Catholics, Protestants, and Muslims
in the past have done to one another across the continent. This in large
part explains Europe's current trend away from organized religion, since
their ancestral psyche is too pock-marked with the failed mergers of
church and state to again validate them with authority. This has also
contributed to a generous cultural will, which ironically has helped
Muslims - some themselves fanatical - immigrate in large numbers.
The subsequent re-introduction of religious stridency and the failure
of a gradual assimilation that's successfully diluted any real flammabil-
ity in the United States' immigrant history has transformed Europe's
newfound tolerance into a new, far more precarious animal.

Europe, too, has something in greater measure than America.
Though it's laid low for over half a century there's a wild imbalance
in European blood that seems to be far more tempered in America.
Domestic or otherwise the United States' most shameful moment is
slavery. This was about as grim as it gets but even there a methodol-
ogy existed that in some ways made it more sinister. The Civil War
exacted enormous losses, but other than the frontier it was fought with

a deliberation and mutual respect not common to internal bloodshed. In the century of racial violence that followed incidents were common, ubiquitous, and brutal, but even then rarely involved more than one killing and were often performed in at least half-secrecy. Beyond slavery, other in-house violence such as labor disputes and a few riots in the sixties was both scattered and low in casualties. Indian abuse is the exception, though it took over two centuries and was at least attended with a modicum of diplomacy, even if that was mostly postured. At peace, ironically, America shows similar restraint. Despite the overall controlled dispatch of its civil violence, America's peace is suffused with a disquieting undercurrent that bridles its respites as much as method and temperance check its turpitude from becoming chaos. We have the highest murder rates, violent crimes, and blood-soaked popular culture of any industrialized nation, and we constantly seem on the brink of war with foreign enemies real or imagined. Rarely, then, if ever, do we hit the extremes either in violence or peace, but rather waver within a narrower continuum. Europe is much different.

Right now they've hit the peace, nearly its endpoint. Worn out after World War II, finally enacting the lofty altruism embedded in their best philosophy, Europe on the whole is internally as placid as powerful people can be. They murder each other, but rarely. Their politics have at times been bitterly divided but often to comic effect, such as British parliamentary procedure. It's in these divisions, however, that the wind is shifting, and Muslims resistant to the tolerance that has finally seemed to settle down in Europe are the agents of change. Having enjoyed a few generations of liberal quietude unknown before on the continent, this disturbing influx has been somewhat coddled. An inability on either side to fully compromise, however, will eventually ignite incidents like the Theo van Gough murder or the recent London bombings on a larger scale. This will trigger the single-minded violence which has made Europe a far more contrasted place than America, when this violence is held up against the liberal ideals Europeans have nobly fostered beside it.

Americans think they know extremity. Conservatives in the sixties and seventies thought the Democrats were a full-blown socialist state. Dogmatic liberals today are convinced Bush is approaching fascism. The truth is, America's an equatorial creature, uncomfortable near the poles. Europe, on the other hand, is purely polar. They may cross the middle en route, but they like the extremes, and they're en route now. Pim Fortuyn remains wildly popular in near martyrdom. He demanded the extradition of Muslims, as did van Gough. Austria's parliament has a creeping Nazi-like entity making gains, as does Italy. France, too, famous for it's spasmodic violence, had a radical right-wing candidate recently force a run-off for prime minister. Even in Sweden - legacy of the Vikings, people not remembered for restraint - white supremacy is making unsettling murmurs. The immigrants feel this shift, and shift in turn from it. Europe's past - that of the Inquisition, witch trials, the Wars of the Roses, the Thirty Year's War, St. Bartholomew's Day, the guillotine, the Franco-Prussian War, the trenches, blitzkrieg, and the Holocaust - will recrudesce, and when it does the violence will come as a shock to most Americans. There's a throttle in this country, a good one. We may head too far in one direction but we back off quickly and redirect. Europe's temperance is less governed. They smash into both extremes, clean themselves up, build a new boat, and head for the other side. Like so many times in their history they're heading that way again. They'll recover - they always do - but it's going to be ugly. It will start quick and end quick. America - handcuffed - will watch, unless of course the Muslim world enters, the results of which will be unknown.

Chapter 12

Keep Your Feet

For a long time America's suit-happy culture has been shifting responsibility from the individual to either a private or corporate entity. This has inevitably produced friction in the populace - between vendor and client, property owner and property user, product manufacturer and product buyer - that has translated itself into political friction as well. Laws, now - specifically in the medical service industry - are being proposed to govern lawyers, or at least limit when they can council a suit and how much they'll receive if they win. From here it's a natural move from the world of doctors to other arenas such as food services, manufacturing, property ownership, and even tobacco companies, as has already been proffered. The Bush administration, however, first presented the suit issue through tort reform, and though I'm displeased with more of this presidency than not I'll not only hear it out on this issue but be more than willing to meet half-way, particularly as it may open other, here-to-fore unseen doors in American culture.

Bush and his people have business backgrounds so I trust they're doing what all purchasing and sales agents do - asking for far more than they actually expect in the hope that haggling will give them what they want. Their proposal is to limit medical damage suits to two-hundred and fifty-thousand dollars while heavily reducing what they call 'frivolous' cases. The medical world - a powerful one - has lobbied hard for this. Doctors went a long way in thwarting Hilary Clinton's national health plan, and probably would've succeeded anyway even had that proposal been remotely comprehensible. Now doctors are claiming they're being driven out of business by malpractice rates, which in turn have dramatically driven up health care costs. Like all lobby groups the doctors here have bloated a kernel of truth into a giant bean-stalk, but they do have a mild point. What they're hiding - or at least choosing not to reveal - is that they themselves aren't perfect. This is one reason some degree of tort reform is necessary - not from the doctors' standpoint so much but the patient's, or at least what I'd like see as a shift in the patient's point-of-view. Though this issue deals both with people's health and their livelihoods it's not without humor, at least for the majority of us who aren't doctors and lawyers. Should tort reform fail the general populace is being asked to feel sorry for doctors and good for lawyers. If it passes, however, we're supposed to do cart-wheels for the long-oppressed medical profession and take a moment of silence for all the poor law firms. Beyond that, though, there's something fundamentally wrong with both the way doctors view themselves and the way many patients view doctors, and from this latter point the country has an opportunity to both re-assess and rectify the disturbing trend of shifting blame from customer to proprietor.

Doctor's aren't miracle workers. Many of them believe they are, and many of those are undeniably gifted. With all our advances in medicine, however, we still can't stop people from either dying or physically breaking down. There may come a day when we live for hundreds of years, but the body - like all things - deteriorates, and while doctors may fight heroic delaying actions nature can only be fought so hard. Many people understand this, but just as many don't; death might be negotiable for a time, but you can't opt out. To compound this irritable fact doctors can't always stave it off. Diseases are tricky, and even a good physician may have occasional trouble diagnosing one in time. Any law suit where a person dies because of dilatory diagnosis, then, is a tough one, as are cases where an operation simply doesn't work. On one hand people are upset because they're either bereft or still in pain and these problems may have been prevented. On the other it must be understood that doctors don't mis-diagnose or botch operations out of malice or an attempt to swindle anyone. They either make mistakes or the body simply can't be mended. Unfortunately, though, for everyone involved, bad things happen in these situations, and it's within this conflict that the tort issue will have its bloodiest battles.

There's also at least one great irony swirling about this conflict. The current Republican Party can count free market competition among the dwindling number of conservative tenets they still defend. Tort reform, however, is a masked but catastrophic abuse of the market free-for-all normally championed by *laissez-faire* strongmen. Law firms may be a lot of things but they're a business first. They make money, huge sums of it, and medical law suits are certainly one way they do it. Doctors are in business as well, and it could be that anyone of them who has been forced to quit because of high insurance or repeated suits was simply a victim of cut-throat market competition rather than any injustices in the courts. In short, they were crummy doctors. For the federal government to step in and protect certain weaker businesses while denying aggressive law firms good revenue would seem counter-intuitive to long-standing conservative tradition. So be it. I personally favor a measure of tort reform, but am happy not to be involved in the details. Doctors make unforgivable errors all the time and people die because of it. Two-hundred and fifty-thousand dollars doesn't seem enough, and the sum should be sufficient to put the fear of God into anyone performing an appendectomy not to sew in a sponge. The particulars, however, can be worked out in Congress. My interest in the issue is conceptual, not specific, and that interest lies in what reform can do for the national consciousness at the individual level.

People blame each other all the time. We all do it, and to a certain extent the aeration is probably healthy. We've been blaming each other for eons, afterall, so it must be. There's a line there, though, that shouldn't be crossed, and a fixation on blame can cause an inward putrefaction within both individuals and entire cultures if it's allowed to fester. This is a particular shame in America since American democracy provides the type of freedoms that promote vigor rather than apathy. Although I'm sure political parties have always accused each other of obstruction along with various abuses of power, this has seemed particularly acute in the last fifty years or so, with the major parties switching which particular brand of blame they lay and which they receive as their altering majorities have dictated. This country's real power, though, lies not in its political parties but within the individual, and it's here where a shift in tort policy could jolt the realization of that power tectonically back to where it rightfully resides - within the citizen.

Perhaps as a reflection of the blame flying around all branches of government these days, citizens themselves seem to be laying more of it than usual at that same government's feet. This habit, in turn, has encouraged foregoing individual choice for the disagreeable trend of blaming the producers of what in fact are for many people irresistible sins. Everything from raunchy television to violent video games to a host of complaints against an abstract unit known as corporate America are for most people now entirely the fault of the producers, as well as the government for not doing anything to stop them. What's been lost is a simple but fundamental fact of not just American life but ideal human life - that no one can make us do anything, particularly in this country. With more political freedoms than just about anywhere in the world, capitalism also gives us a great deal of power over those seeking our money. People have forgotten this, and though there are many contributing factors, the reliance on both government and powerful corporations to make decisions for us is prominent among them, as is the notion to blame these people when those decisions are either ineffective or displeasing. The tort issue exemplifies this. At some point, of course, it's true, we all need a doctor. People in the main, though, live so unhealthily in this country that medical attention is many times over what it needs to be. We smoke a lot, eat bad food, and live lives somewhere between sedentary and catatonic. In other words, we're fat and out of shape and many people simply assume doctor's visits and prescription drugs should by right-of-birth cure whatever ails them. If it doesn't then a law suit is considered not only an option but an obligation, and this mindset translates at least obliquely to other fields.

Television is an easy one. For a decade or more people of all stripes have condemned the rise of bad programming, most recently the deluge of reality TV. Blame has rested almost entirely on the purveyors of this trash, and many fingers are now being pointed at the FCC to control them. While curbing these programs as they currently stand would come dangerously close to intrusive censorship that's beside the point. People need to remember that production houses are in business for the same reason everyone else is - to make money. They won't make shows that people won't watch, and right now the fact is that trash sells. The solution, however, is simple. Don't' watch. If people are so appalled by what's on television they can simply make the choice either not to view it or prevent their kids from watching. As soon as ratings slip and advertisers stop paying large sums for time slots, the show will be pulled. The same is true of the often banal and mass-produced tripe coming out of Hollywood - don't go to the movies and eventually the production companies will make the correct business decision to market what people are in fact willing to see. Video games are the same. If you don't like what your kids play, don't let them play it. The FCC should have nothing to do with what individuals can change for themselves.

The same is conceptually true of corporate America, the blanket term for a loosely defined set of large companies that receive blame for everything from environmental degradation to job outsourcing to manipulating markets to making a whitewash of American culture. This one's a little trickier, since many of these companies - such as oil producers - make products we all need to one extent or another, but the formula still holds to a certain degree - buy only what you absolutely need and look for alternatives. Wal-Mart is useful for one purpose and one purpose only - it sells a lot of stuff and it sells it cheap. Sometimes we need certain items and can only afford so much. The downsides of these mega-stores, however, are enormous. They not only send jobs - good ones, anyway - overseas, but the products that come back are a fraction of the quality that American companies once produced. It used to be you could buy a Stanley wrench set where each piece had enough torque to manage even the rustiest nut and a durability that insured your grandchildren would be giving those same tools to their kids. The same wrench set from China, on the other hand, may be a third of the cost or less but has half the strength of the Stanley set and you'll be lucky to hand one of them to the next generation for all the bending and breaking that'll occur. The same with oil and other energy sources. If you don't like the way this company or that treats the environment, do your best not to buy that producer's product. Even a few conscious decisions a year by each individual will make an enormous difference. Companies only produce what people buy. If enough people stop or lessen their buying, then, any problems caused by either the product or the company will either be greatly mitigated or disappear altogether.

Should tort reform pass even to a degree my great joy will not be for the doctors, who are no doubt not scrounging as advertised. It will be the hope that people can be knocked back into realizing they should put more onus on themselves for the direction of both their own lives and that of the country's. This doesn't entirely shift accountability by any measure. The government, corporations, and property owners should all unequivocally be held to task for their actions, their decisions, and the considerable powers they possess. But by taking more responsibility for their own actions and decisions citizens can go a long way in returning a portion of that power back in the individual where it belongs. Years ago I had a friend who's parents owned a deli in South Philadelphia. They'd immigrated from Italy and worked themselves silly for that business. There'd been a cold snap and some guy slipped on a patch of sidewalk ice out front. Apparently the business owner is responsible for that. The guy cracked an ankle and received an absurd amount of money over an absurd period of time. While I'll certainly agree that the store owner's should pay the medical bills, enough is enough when it comes to crippling somebody financially because they missed a little slick patch with the rock salt. The guy was walking on ice and should've known it. In other words, next time keep your feet.

Chapter 13

The Watershed

Universal health care would add a tremendous chunk to the federal government. In that, at least, there's no doubt. If this is good to some and abhorrent to others, it taps something common in all of us, for though we say we don't most of us like big government in selective spheres while proudly hating it in others. Mostly, of course, we favor the latter. Outside a few liberals of the European model, most Americans feel a shared sense of duty to denounce Washington's role in their personal lives. It's a duplicity that pervades everyone. If some people hate the government nosing in on their privacy, they might like the idea of broader welfare and expanded public education. Conversely, if another person detests welfare and supports school vouchers, they might tout a protracted military and closer ties between church and state. The good news is as a people and as individuals we can claim both for and against strong government and still live with ourselves, for it's a paradox superceded by a simple truth, running along the spine of the word freedom, itself a tricky word - over-used, widely interpreted, and never understood. Abe Lincoln, though he substituted the word liberty, said the world had never had a good definition of it. "We all declare for liberty," he said, "but in using the same word, we do not mean the same thing." Although at the time attempting to reconcile different beliefs on slavery, his declaration regarding the difficulties in defining freedom is as relevant now as it was then, for if any one thing truly separates people in this country it's the watershed spilling on either side of our shared love of freedom. If individuals, then, can in fact be defined by the terms liberal and conservative that definition comes from on what side of the divide they most often end up. Every issue - from foreign policy to education to Social Security - finds a person on one side or the other, and if the two camps - liberal and conservative - can't understand each other, it's less for the mountain range that stands between them than for the fervent desire of freedom they once shared atop that same range. Time, and what people choose to do with it, is often the factor deciding which valley they'll tumble into, for by any definition governance of our own time is our most powerful claim to freedom, and for me a national health plan would be sanctioned if for no other reason than the gift of time it would grant us.

No matter how long you live it isn't very long. That's a favorite saying of my father's and as I've grown older it's become a favorite of mine as well. None of us - not even the very sickly - literally live every moment like it might be our last, which is a shame given how little time we actually have. A forty-four year old friend of mine - a math whiz - once told me that he'd calculated he had twelve thousand hours left to live. That rattled me. No matter the context, no matter what you compare it to, that number sounds like what it is - a pittance. Our time, then, is nothing less than sacred, and the more freedom we have in choosing what to do with it the better. All of us, of course, have different pursuits. Time spent under a car for one is time better spent at the park for another. Where one person pours over stock reports, the guy next door pours over box scores, and so on. No one, however, not even the oddest among us, considers filling out HMO paperwork or fretting over which health plan has the best hand bone coverage as the most fulfilling use of our limited time. For most of us - myself included - such wrangling is an outright absurdity, right up there with pounding nails with your forehead, and buoyed by some traditional supports is the chief reason why I strongly favor universal medical coverage.

For many, obviously, this is anathema. For me, given the colossal waste of time people devote of necessity to petty insurance dickering, it's one of the more lucid issues of the current political climate. Other commonly heard arguments, of course, abound, and most of those are bullet-proof. Sentiment, though, isn't among them. While the fact that so many people are uninsured and so many of those are little kids is both a national embarrassment and a personal heart-tug, sentiment alone rarely makes good policy. Comparisons, however, do. Europe and Canada have national health care. American dissenters claim these nations pay more through higher taxes while receiving poorer care, but numbers show otherwise. Americans pay higher per capita health care and live shorter lives than those in most countries with public health service. Additionally, while citizens in these countries may have high taxes, companies don't, at least when it comes to health insurance. American employers, on the other hand, are anywhere from burdened to outright stifled by these costs. In fact, it's near certain that health benefits alone drive many business owners overseas. Entrepreneurship suffers as well. Many people in urgent need of health insurance often pursue middling jobs with some sort of coverage rather than devoting their time to innovation and starting new businesses. All these reasons are well known and collectively sound enough for many people to sanction a national medical plan. To me they make sense, as well, but alongside time and the freedom that comes with it these reasons are simply props.

Everybody's different. This is why the watershed needs to be revisited with each issue. Concerning things like gun control, foreign wars, religion, and personal privacy, in most cases I want government influence to be anywhere from small to non-existent. In other arenas, such as public education, environmental law, and anti-trust policies, I'm on the other side, where government can't get big enough. Health care is the same way, though millions of people obviously have a different perspective, even when it comes to the single factor of freedom. As always, interpretation of that word makes the difference. For some, freedom in health services means the freedom to choose your own care. That used to mean picking the doctor with whom you were most comfortable. More and more, of course, it means deciding which coverage suits you best, which often influences what job you take. Nowadays, the doctor you get is most times chosen by the carrier, not the individual, but a great many people are still pleased with fact that they - and not the government - have more sway in who takes care of them. This feeling is not without merit, and being leery if not loathe of expanded government in many areas myself it's certainly something I understand. In the case of health care, however, it's not one I support, for beside the increasing illusion that individuals govern their own medical treatment and the exponential cost of private care versus public, the time involved in the labyrinth of modern health insurance is far more than I can bear.

I hear it all the time - from friends, family, people at work. A sickness or injury pops up and off they go to the doctor. After deciding with various insurance functionaries who they can see, they fill out the proper paperwork with medical aides prior to any initial screening. Upon receiving whatever treatment they need a minor but ugly little war inevitably arises over who pays for what. Given what Americans and their employers pay in health insurance, it's understood by no one but well-paid actuaries why patients pay much of anything at all. That, however, is of secondary importance to me. My business is with time. Like most people I'm terribly greedy with my own time. Sickness or injury cuts into it, of course, which is bad enough but often inevitable. The last thing in the world I want is to waste more time haggling with an insurance carrier for great lengths over what I should or shouldn't pay. This can take hours, days, or even weeks. The fact that I'll lose most of that battle most of the time is a double loss - I lose out on money, another precious commodity, but more importantly I lose a great deal of time, by far the greater loss. On the other hand, were the government to pick up the tab, even if I eventually pay an equal share through higher taxes I gain mightily in simply being fixed by a doctor and from there am able to do with my time as I please. I walk in, get treatment, and leave - maybe with a limp, maybe with a nagging cough, but, from there on out, in full possession of my time.

Americans have a bad habit of chest-beating, which leads us to bloat our qualities to outrageous proportions. While this is a shame it's also a natural by-product, for the truth is as a nation we do have some very fine qualities. Like most people we love freedom. Through the constitution, however, I believe freedom's elusive concept has been provided a better framework than anywhere else, and subsequently our citizens enjoy a great deal more of it than in other places. We also have a genius for synthesis, a gift we rarely if ever acknowledge. Starting with the constitution itself Americans have often taken the best of ideas from far-ranging sources and woven them into a greater whole. Maybe health care can work the same. We love government and we hate it. We also love choice. From this perhaps a system can be orchestrated where doctors who choose to do so can work outside the government system, providing care to those who wish to stand outside it as well. Alongside this, though, would be a federal provider, based largely on models in Canada and Europe. This would replace both Medicare and Medicaid. Whatever their reasons, people could choose this system as well. Though we don't all attend them, we all pay for public schools. Health care could be the same. Choice, then, could be had by all, and though we'd stand back atop the divide with different definitions of freedom, we'd no longer - at least on this one issue - stand blinded to each other in two different watersheds. That would be a compromise, our first and most durable talent as a people.

Chapter 14

The Shackle and the Bolt-Cutter

Two American folk songs encapsulate the contrary influences that history will have on a culture. *Yankee Doodle*, from the Revolution, represents history's role as dismissible trivia, whereas *Marching Through Georgia*, penned late in the Civil War, embodies the solemn sense of obligation a shared past can instill in a people. The Iraq War shows a measure of both, where those who launched it pushed aside any historical impediments such as non-pre-emption while simultaneously becoming suffused with a maudlin interpretation of America's past and largely honorable role as the purveyor of various freedoms. In each example the Bush administration respectively liberated itself from history's millstone through the *Yankee Doodle* approach while shackling its policies to that same weight by way of the *Georgia* route. How the future will unfold from this confluence is unknown, though personally I think the war's most beneficial aim - that of shifting the Middle East away from religious oligarchs and toward democracy - could have been accomplished by shepherding the inertia that was already tilted that way. Bush himself, though, said early on one of the more intelligent things of his own or any presidency. When asked how history will judge the Iraq War he answered, "I don't know, we'll all be dead," and while he took sharp criticism for this he was right. No one living knows what the war's long-term effects will be. As things stand now, they could go either way. We simply don't know, and won't for a generation or more. I won't, then, speculate on how the war will be received in the future, but it's both useful and necessary to sort out how the Bush people selectively neglected and embraced history in order to start the conflict in the first place.

On the one hand I admire the *Yankee Doodle* approach, as it's as American as the song itself. Like many aspects of the Revolution what's fact and what's myth is unknown, but from what we have of it the song certainly has an interesting origin. When the colonists initiated combat they weren't considered an independent country but rebels without a history of their own. In many ways this reflected the character of the upstarts themselves, as many people living here had migrated from somewhere else largely to forget their own checkered pasts. Once here they could start anew. The British, on the other hand, were proudly ingrained by history, and mocked the American's lack of a structured, gloried past. In their own turn the Americans mocked back, showing a scorn for history through new lyrics to an old tune. Taking a British melody, a sarcastic colonist crafted for it nonsensical rhymes to deliberately chide the venerable regard with which Britons held their own ancestry. Even today, everyone knows the lines:

> *Yankee Doodle went to town*
> *A-ridin' on a pony*
> *Stuck a feather in his cap*
> *And called it macaroni*

America, as the English pointed out, didn't have a history, and the aim of *Yankee Doodle's* author was that it didn't care. History was for old men stodging about picnic tables, nursing their pints and chess boards while reveling in past glories. If a people as a whole paid undue homage to the past it made for hesitation and inaction when action was what was needed. The colonists wanted emancipation from British tyranny. If they got caught up in what the English thought was owed them through a shared history then they'd likely never act toward what many at the time and most today consider a great push forward for mankind's overall liberty. Americans at the time, then, didn't have a history, which freed them to make one of their own. Regarding Iraq, Bush and his people obviously admired this approach as well. In early 2003 - two-hundred and twenty-seven years after declared independence - America not only had a history but a storied one. While the war touters within the administration chose to adopt some of it, they were highly selective, choosing equally to ignore three of that same history's most respected pillars - pre-emptive war, foreign distractions, and the glaring anomaly of cutting taxes during war time.

The taxes I'll leave alone, as I believe that issue speaks for itself. If there's a wisdom in not asking citizens to pay for a war ostensibly waged to protect them, then that wisdom will have to be revealed in the future. The other two, pre-emption and foreign distractions, are related. Whether it's self-appointed or not is debatable, but America is and always has been imbued with a sense of justice, which for many means divine justice. Pre-emptive war, then, has never sat right with us. Attacking another people simply because we feel they might be a threat has historically been an unsettling concept, and to do so a split with our judicial covenant. Of course our history is flush with debatable examples of pre-emption, but they're debatable because certain administrations may or may not have engineered circumstances to make the other side draw first blood. If such contrivances were made, they were made because past presidents understood the presiding American loathing of foreign conflict. It's certainly plausible, for example, that Polk arranged matters as such that Mexico had to strike first. The *USS Maine* will forever be shrouded in mystery, as well, as will Frank Roosevelt's possible set-up of Pearl Harbor. The Gulf of Tonkin, on the other hand, has been all but proven a fraud. Though conspiracy theorists on the far, Marxist-soaked left will always believe that the Bushies let the 9/11 hi-jackers in, such an accusation is prudently ignored by most. The fact, however, that we pre-empted Iraq based on sketchy and even doctored intelligence is now disputed only by the extreme right, themselves steeped in the opaque calculus of Leo Strauss, a figure whose legacy may prove every bit as toxic as Marx's. The Bush administration, then, considered Iraq a potential threat and attacked without at any attempt to gull the other side into hitting first, which marks a distinct break with the past. History was ignored or even shunned, in other words, in order to orchestrate a new history.

Equally ignored but less an historical rift was the Iraq invasion's counter-weight to America's disdain of distractions beyond its own borders. Though presidents of every stripe have used minor engagements abroad to mask or promote varied agendas - Reagan in Grenada, Bush in Panama, Wilson in Mexico, Clinton in Somalia - this country's governing aim has been to defend the homeland and let the rest of the world fiddle with its own affairs. Washington warned of involvement with 'foreign entanglements', while Quincy Adams stated that 'monsters' shouldn't be sought abroad. A great portion of the country - including most of William McKinley's fellow Civil War veterans - despised both him and Teddy Roosevelt for their imperial meddling in Cuba and the Philippines. Many hated Clinton for Kosovo. Bush, then, isn't the first to sink both American troops and funds in a foreign war not overwhelmingly supported by the public. Any president that does this, however, is upsetting the country's traditional will if not its history. If we fight on foreign soil often, we don't like it, and consider any such endeavor an exception to our preference for business and diplomacy when engaging other nations. Bush - combining pre-emption with this latest breach of the foreign distraction tradition - did one of two things. Either he knew so little of history - which is absurd - that by invading Iraq he had no idea he was countermanding much of it, or - by far the more plausible - he knew the history and cared nothing for it, crafting a *Yankee Doodle* of his own.

If Iraq turns out well, if some early indications of the Middle East's lean toward democracy come to fruition, I'll forgive Bush's willful break with history even though I think it could've been accomplished through other means. I see it as requiring forgiveness only because at heart I'm an isolationist, not caring to expend American blood in an effort to change other people. I like the idea of tending your own plot and leaving the neighbors to theirs unless they're in dire emergency. Rwanda, in other words, I feel would've merited our involvement, as did the recent Asian tsunami, and while I'm certainly glad we joined the World Wars I admire our abstaining from them as long as possible. I don't believe in pre-emption and I don't believe it's our job to remove dictators operating within their own borders, however detestable they may be. For this reason I'll never - no matter how the Middle East turns out - forgive the Bush administration for their *Marching Through Georgia* approach to history.

For a long time people denied slavery's primacy as the Civil War's leading cause, including Abraham Lincoln publicly. By late 1864, however, as Sherman's army marched south from Atlanta, the soldiers could see it. They walked nearly unopposed through Georgia's heart - burning homes, thieving crops, freeing slaves. Many of the blacks had run off by then, but the many who hadn't reveled in the Union arrival. The looks on their faces - true emancipation written in visceral, human expression - affected the whites that saw them. We now know that most northern soldiers cared little for the slaves, with many disdaining blacks as much as the southerners whom they fought did. Still, though, with the joy of the newly freed all around them, they knew they were having a profound impact on history, so much so that even the most prejudiced heart must've been somewhat alleviated. One soldier wrote a song, forgotten now, describing this sensation, a history-altering one granted to people who free others:

> *Ring the good ol' bugle, boys, we'll sing another song*
> *Sing it with a spirit that will start the world along*
> *Sing it as we used to sing it fifty-thousand strong*
> *While we were marching through Georgia*
>
> *How the darkies shouted when they heard the joyful sound*
> *How the turkeys gobbled which our commissary found*
> *How the sweet potatoes nearly started from the ground*
> *While we were marching through Georgia*
>
> *Hurrah, Hurrah, we bring the Jubilee*
> *Hurrah, Hurrah, the flag that makes you free*
> *So we sang the chorus from Atlanta to the sea*
> *While we were marching through Georgia*

Along with the word 'darky' the 'hurrahs' and simple rhymes antiquate this piece. That's unfortunate, for it catches perfectly in words the emotion recently confiscated by the Republican Party, turning a once conservative bastion - abhorrent of spendy foreign wars with lofty ambitions - into a dewy-eyed, utopian congress. It's this piece of history that Bush's people have whole-heartedly bought into, and subsequently sold with equal vigor to the American public. Freeing people from tyranny is not a concept I oppose. I am, however, against its role in the Iraq War on three points - location, method, and tone, all of which are tangential in this particular case.

I'm not much of a sentimentalist. *Marching Through Georgia*, though, hits a soft chord in me the same way it does the current war's supporters. Being American, I'm generally fond of the place and its history, but it's the country's great idea I worship most - that of a people freed to rule themselves and dictate their own happiness. In my eyes the Constitution is one of the greatest documents ever written. If I admire its political tenets, however, it's more for the philosophy that underpins them. Through the Civil War the glaring hypocrisy of the Constitution - as reflected by the society that produced it - saw a great tearing-down, and that crumbling is enshrined in *Georgia's* simple lyrics. Slavery was the country's seminal stain, and the ones who removed it were deservedly infused with a sense of grace, where even the potatoes seemed to rise from the earth in support. Bush and I, though, as much as we'd be united by the song's theme of spreading freedom, would be equally at odds on one line, but it's a substantial disagreement.

Slavery was an in-house problem. America's founding generation designed the best governing system to date, but knew they'd heired a heap of inconsistencies to posterity. Thankfully, many of those problems have been erased. In a hundred year's time - from about 1820 - 1920 - the landless could vote, slaves were freed and could vote, and women, finally, were granted the vote as well. Also during this time bloody rhetoric in Washington mirrored the often bloody labor disputes in the rest of the country, but finally business owners and laborers came to an acceptable if tense understanding. In all these struggles and their ensuing triumphs people suffered and sacrificed in order to elevate America toward its grand ideal. It's an ideal in which I fervently believe and most certainly want other countries to share in - a noble if somewhat arrogant wish pervading most Americans. In *Georgia* that desire comes in the line *"sing it with a spirit that will start the world along"*, though it's in those words' interpretation where both the Iraq War's supporters and detractors - people who equally want freedom to spread - passionately part.

In my eyes it's America's job to take care of itself by living up to our highest standards as granted by the Constitution. More than laws, that document places human reason at the center of society's construction alongside the freedoms for citizens in a given age to decide for themselves what constitutes the ethical mores of a particular time. While I want these concepts ubiquitous around the globe I also believe in leadership through example rather than force. We have a great system, and particularly in the age of information and rapid travel that system is easily observed. Prior to our invasion of Iraq many in the Middle East had taken notice and were working - however slowly - to press against tyranny if not to outright champion democracy. Organic change usually makes a far more agreeable and permanent revolution than one that's imposed, though there are, of course, exceptions. Germany and Japan had democracy forced on them and are doing quite well, whereas the French Revolution came from within and was by all counts a disaster. The French, however, didn't have a model. The U.S. was only a few years old and itself scrambling to define democracy, while Germany and Japan had gone grossly outside their borders in horrific ways and were only transformed after being reduced to ashes. In those cases I'm all for force. Iraq, though, was different. Hussein was an awful man. In my and many opinions, though, it was up to the Iraqi people to overthrow him. American energy - including funds and blood - should be generated inward to ensure the highest liberty available at home, and expended outward only in regard to business, diplomacy, and the exchange of ideas, which often are one and the same. It's this example that will start the world along. Bush, though, and the war's supporters, interpret that line quite differently. They've transformed the obligation to guarantee freedom within our own bounds into a self-appointed responsibility to impose it elsewhere. The army of "fifty-thousand strong", in other words, has moved abroad, and - except in extreme cases like World War II - whether or not it has any place there is essentially the crux of not only the Iraq debate but Bush's vision as stated in his second inaugural.

The current administration, then, used history as both a shackle and bolt-cutter in order to launch the Iraq War. Adopting the same tack the colonists took through *Yankee Doodle*, Bush abandoned historical orthodoxy by pre-empting a purported foreign enemy without any pretense that they'd hit first. An expensive endeavor, he did this by cutting rather than raising taxes, a move without precedent. Conversely, the war's designers also chained themselves to the American historical tradition of emancipation, or at least their version of it. Similar to the author of the long-ago *Marching Through Georgia,* the Bush people have taken the American flag as that which "makes you free". They have, though, gone a highly controversial step beyond that, taking for their Georgia the Middle East. In the one America had an urgent responsibility to manumit its own slaves, while in the other it's unclear we had any responsibility at all. 9/11, of course, created its own urgency. If Iraq continues toward democracy and surrounding countries creep ahead with similar transitions, I'll have to abide Bush's *Yankee Doodle* doctrine, given that the war's expense doesn't further jeopardize us financially. It's my great hope, though, that our insistence upon forced democracy ends with Iraq, because like many Americans both living and dead I don't feel the country's obligation to spread freedom extends to foreign wars that cost us in both blood and money, though there are exceptions in extreme, out-of-border threats. The Taliban was crippled in Afghanistan and al-Qaeda severely damaged. Installing democracy there I felt unquestionably justified, as the Taliban was a ruthless foreign occupier and al-Qaeda undeniably responsible for 9/11. The combination of our own humility and the example of democracy in Afghanistan, I believe, would've triggered the substantial democratic populism that was already stirring beneath Middle Eastern tyranny, especially in secular Iraq. Assuming the role of democratic enforcer beyond our own boundaries, however - even should it eventually work - is not a role I want for this country, and for that reason I'll always begrudge George Bush and his *Georgian* interpretation of international American influence.

Chapter 15

Common Sense and the Environment

The environment - or at least the stress put on it by human beings - is for many people a common sense issue. This might make it simple if it weren't so complicated, for there's two types of common sense, sometimes in conflict, that often govern our views. There's personal common sense, an angle that seems obvious to you and either a majority or minority of varying size, and at-large common sense, things that are clear to nearly everyone. Sometimes the two fuse well, making an issue easy. Nuclear warfare is one. It's bad for you, bad for me, bad for everybody. No one holds the other position. Unfortunately, most topics aren't that clear, for if the at-large common sense is shared by most, personal common sense can split people into several factions. In addition, this more interpretive brand of perception can itself fracture within an individual, causing several different views in the same person. These problems compound prolifically when the at-large common sense of one major issue comes in conflict with that of another, as seemingly happens with the environment and the global economy. It can make a mess, and in the end all someone can do is speak for themselves. For me, the combined common sense concerning the environment - personal and at-large - aligns in such a way as to overwhelmingly favor both conservation and a radical shift in how we impact the earth. Even with that said, however, problems arise, for environmental issues are so intimately entwined with other concerns that conflicts seem pre-ordained. No matter what we do, in other words, we're going to have an impact, for we need to extract and use resources not only to live comfortably but to live at all. Still, though, from both a broader common sense view as well as a personal, less palpable one, it's clear to me that we have to mitigate our inevitable effects on the earth while preserving what we still have of undeveloped land, and we need to do so very soon.

Geniuses and Fools Alike - At-Large Common Sense

There's a great deal of at-large common sense to the environment that's often obscured by its obviousness, and in this it shares with many things, fitness among them. For all the doctors' reports, dietary fads, and workout hypes that cycle through, most people know that if you eat moderately and exercise regularly you're going to stay relatively healthy. Bacon-cheeseburgers may kill you today and save you tomorrow while this or that ab regimen goes in and out of style, but simple common sense tells you that a burger here and there won't harm you as long as you burn it off, however you choose to do it. If you can't grate cheese on your stomach, you'll nevertheless be just as resistant to heart trouble, high blood pressure, and simple lethargy as the workout freak next to you. Scientists and other experts can certainly refine common sense, then, and may even illuminate new aspects of it that weren't readily apparent before, but they don't much change its basic shape, which for anyone willing to see it usually lies in plain sight.

The political, physical, and social ferment surrounding the environment can be a lot like contemplating god, with some of it too big, too much, to attempt grasping, while other aspects seem more approachable. Though global warming is by all means a concern for me, there's too much there to warrant daily preoccupation, since I can't fully comprehend either its causes or future effects. That it's occurring couldn't be more obvious, but whether we're the primary mover or what the results of curbing our environmental practices in order to thwart it would be I have no idea. It's most likely a natural cycle that we've exacerbated mightily, but the exact truth will probably never be known. As a phenomenon, in the meantime, it's well on its way by now, and any effort on our part to reverse it would likely do very little. These same efforts would, though, address other environmental issues that not only are of urgent concern to me but at least one of which - toxins - should collectively jolt everyone's at-large common sense, since the levels of man-made filth in the air, water, and soil are among our clearest-cut present-day catastrophes.

There is, of course, an awareness-shortage with toxins, the chief of which is that you can't see them. Outside of certain smog pockets or the occasional chemical spill, what pollutes our environment and therefore our bodies is largely invisible to the naked eye. It's also slow-working, or at least slower than other dangers that grip so many of us with profound fear. Unlike car bombers or anthrax threats, for instance, toxic effects aren't normally immediate - there's no dramatic explosion or bodies stacked up behind hospital morgues to ignite both fear and passion. When it's PCB's or dioxins that kill you they kill you over many years, where you eventually weaken, enter a hospital, and die there, the cause of your illness probably never determined. Such deaths happen all the time, but since they take place quietly, tucked away in cancer wards all around the globe, we put it out of our minds, in spite of the fact that common sense should tell us better, as the danger of humanity's collective industrial output is by now absent of mystery.

Over the last three centuries we've put untold amounts of sulfur, carbon dioxide, mercury, lead, and other ill-bred particles into the environment - the air we breathe, the soil we cultivate, the water we drink. There's a disconnect, though, operating in the spheres of visibility and economics, that blinds us to that danger's urgency. Outside those spheres the obvious remains obvious. Everyone knows, in other words, that if you cracked open a dozen thermometers and downed a shot of mercury you'd die in a terrible way. When you lock yourself in a garage and turn on a car you may die in peace but you die all the same. Sulfur isn't any better than lead, and so on. The trouble is, apart from suicides we're not exposed to pollutants in this way. They accrue over a lifetime, through the necessary functions of our lives. We don't see car exhaust but we breathe it. Tomatoes, corn, and beef may look and taste fine, but they imbibe the same cadmium, sulfur, and mercury that we take in when we eat them. These toxins get in our sustenance through the air and the rain, and over time they pile up in us to dangerous levels, especially in young women hoping to give birth. Again, the slightest shred of common sense tells anyone that a woman packed with mercury and other corrosive material has a greater chance of delivering an unhealthy kid than a cleaner mother. It's bad enough that painfully obvious deductions such as this are shielded by toxic invisibility and the lack of sudden, dramatic deaths. An even greater wall, however - the economy, built on a foundation of common sense itself - obstructs it far more.

It's a funny word, economy, a broad term broadly defined, and the complications magnify when it's paired with its sibling term ecology, itself kin to environment. The great irony of polluting the environment is that what kills us - technology fueled by a dynamic economy - also makes us immensely comfortable and wealthy. In addition, energy consumption and its by-products spur pharmaceutical research and medical practices, making it a great healer even as it's a great killer. All of it - the poor health effects, the high standards of living, the filthy rivers, the filthy skies, the state-of-the-art medical industry - are all different, often competing strands in a single entity called the economy, itself a chimera of conflicting common sense codes. Nowadays we think of the economy as the system of market interactions that sustains our financial structures and therefore our civilization. On the surface, of course, that's true. Beneath this dry, grotesquely vague definition, however, are other meanings vital to an understanding of how these elusive numbers and theories are little more than symbols for the way we ourselves interact with the earth - or our environment - in order to maintain our lives. Economy, then, essentially means the management and use of resources, while money is simply a symbol for those same resources, and the extraction, harvest, and processing of them the subsequent juncture of source and symbol. Economics isn't the study of the ebbs and flows of money, therefore, so much as it's the study of how human beings derive their existence from their surroundings, and in this light we're faced with the dilemma of maintaining a healthy economy while simultaneously maintaining a healthy environment. It's not easy business, but all indicators are that it will be far more prudent - from a common sense angle - to adapt our economy to favor the environment rather than expect the environment to adapt to our economy. This is pronounced further now that cleaner technologies seem so near to us. While it's certain that other problems will arise with solar power, cleaner-burning coal, wind and tidal energies, and new fuels such as bio-diesel, it's equally certain that they'll be far less vexing than the centuries' long rampage wrought by the largely unstemmed use of fossil fuels.

Among this blend of hopeful logic lies another rich vein of common sense, countermanding another, less convincing one. A well-known argument against an aggressive overhaul of our industrial practices is that it would be too damaging to the economy - an onerous threat attended by social maladies of its own, real enough to at first make any call against change appear valid. It must be remembered, though, that about a hundred years ago we made a similar transition that didn't take terribly long. At the end of the nineteenth century the economy was fueled by hay, wood, coal, and steam. Twenty years later the majority of it ran on oil, and even by the most liberal analysis the full transition didn't take more than three generations. Things not only didn't collapse, of course, they got better. Jobs weren't lost but created. If the grandparents felled timber, built wagons, and grew hay for horses, grandchildren worked in auto plants, built pipelines, and sold machinery. They also got rich, and there's no reason to believe the same switch-over can't take place now. If people build fewer generators and internal combustion engines, then, they'll construct more fuel cells and solar panels. The economy - or how we use our environment in order to sustain and improve our lives - won't devolve but improve, and in doing so will make the earth a cleaner place. This is an imperative stride. In my home state of Connecticut the game regulations now tell you outright not to eat more than a fish or two a month and to stay away from the organs of white-tail deer altogether. Such warnings are standard. At-large common sense - the collective intuition of geniuses, fools, and everyone in between - tells anyone that what piles up in fish and deer piles up in other foods as well, and if it kills them it'll kill you too. The same is true of what's currently in the air, water, and soil. The means to change all this are at hand, and these strategies quash the far more feeble common sense stance that any such transition will be ruinous to the economy and therefore to us. Nobody dislikes the word behooves. It behooves us, then, to move both collectively and as individuals toward the rapid adoption of more healthful and prosperous methods when utilizing our natural resources.

The Last of It - Personal Common Sense

Gordon Lightfoot, *sui generis*. We'll underestimate him at our peril. If the big Albertan lacks the staying power of Shakespeare or the depth of Melville, he wrote a song, *The Canadian Railroad Trilogy*, that exacts the manifold environmental problems facing us today, particularly one which affects the divergence of personal common sense currently pervading the nation. As far as westward expansion goes, Canadians share our history, and a transcontinental railroad was pivotal. It's a long song, starting this way:

> *There was a time in this fair land when the railroad did not run*
> *When the wild majestic mountains stood alone against the sun*
> *Long before the white man and long before the wheel*
> *When the green dark forest was too silent to be real*
>
> *But time has no beginning and history has no bound*
> *As to this verdant country they came from all around*
> *They sailed upon her waters and walked the forest tall*
> *They built the mines, the mills, and the factories for the good of us all*

It goes on to extol the laborers who sweated and died developing the civilization that now gives us so much comfort. Interspersed with the praise, however, is lament, a deep melancholy for what's been lost in building that civilization. It's a dichotomy that afflicts a great many of us while being wholly absent in many others. For a portion of the population, then, it's the mines, the mills, and the factories that are important, nothing else. Nature is simply here for our use and in an undeveloped, un-manicured state it's not only of no value but in many cases disturbing - a notion running back to the country's origins. For the rest of us, the issue is greatly conflicted. While it's understood that resources are needed and land must be developed, there's an equal desire to preserve all of the 'green dark forest' that we're able, and companion emotions ranging from sadness to rage at the continual disappearance of untrammeled land. This is the hell of personal common sense, for very often it runs against itself within the same individual. Nevertheless - though I personally fully understand the importance of development

95

and industry on many levels - I think for the most part we've got close to enough, and outside punching in the occasional mine and the continued if more intelligent harvest and use of timber and oil, we need to secure all we can of our dwindling tracts of undeveloped land, while fostering all the green space available in the places that are otherwise overrun. These desires, fortunately, are shared by a greater percentage of the country than is generally understood, however diverse their inspirations may be.

In political arguments there are very few presidents safe to reference without appearing biased. Teddy Roosevelt, though, is one. A darling of conservatives and progressives alike, he also had a personal make-up as marbled as any individual you'll find, at times being a raging monster - as in the Philippines and Latin America - and at others being quite compassionate - as in his stands against big business when it came to labor and the overall health of the population. He's also a towering figure in the American environmental movement, a cause in recent decades falsely associated more with saccharin sentiment than the original balance of conservation and development typified by pioneers like Aldo Leopold and Roosevelt himself. That was a mistake foisted in equal parts by the marketing schemes of industry and the overtly romantic views of nature held mostly by people disconnected from it. For his own part, Roosevelt's desire for conservation was driven by a mixture consistent with his overall personality, a mixture passed on to many people today. On the one hand, he earned his legacy as a killer. Snuffing as many critters as he could in a day was a passion with him, and more woods means more critters. His love of wilderness went well beyond this, however, for Roosevelt knew of nature what countless human beings know of it, and in my opinion he deserves a mark of greatness for this knowledge alone.

Already a champion of national parks, Roosevelt also established the national forest system. He did so for two reasons, disparate in character but wedded by the oblique inconsistencies of human need. The country, he knew, would always need natural resources, with trees and minerals high among them. In order for these to endure generation to generation, he understood human nature too well to entrust them to private ownership. He was right. To this day publicly managed land is in far better shape and resource-wise will be consistently more productive than privately held plots. Braided with this openly pragmatic need for conservation, however, was a less tangible though no less critical source for Roosevelt's motives - the multifarious effects the natural world has upon human beings.

The woods do things to people, many things. Whether it's terror or adoration, artistic stimulus or bloodlust, loathing or purification, nature at one point or another moves every emotion in our constitution, often several at once, and as such is a tremendous contemplative source. In addition, being generally absent of other people, it's entirely unique in that it that puts the self squarely within the natural world, a place by now both intimately familiar and fearfully alien to us. It's where we come from, where we take our food and shelter from, and yet we're ourselves increasingly removed from it. Inside this confluence of opposites individuals are alone in a place at once highly kinetic and doggedly fixed. Whether you go there to hunt or paint, float a river or draw a landscape in verse, pick raspberries or simply take a walk, you reach aspects of yourself, humanity, and the world at-large wholly inaccessible in other places. Within this considerable range, of course, is the concept of god. Nothing is more silent than how the world came to be and what if any of its purposes are, and nature is unique in being entirely devoid of both human language and construct. It's also our lone physical conduit to the ethereal. Lightfoot called it 'too silent to be real', but that's wrong and he knew it. Roosevelt knew it, too, and moved desperately to sanctify nature for these reasons. It's silent to our ear, but nothing could be more real.

If you're new to it, April in Alaska surprises everyone. It surprised me too. Like other places, it's a month of great awakening. If buds are still locked in their branches and snows still common, a great many other signs appear marking winter's dissolution. Light, for one, finally overtakes the dark. In the rain forests of southeast Alaska the dismal seven-hour days of weak sunlight are a memory by April, and with the increasing light the winter wrens perk up, scolding high in the dripping spruce boughs for the first time in months. The season's first thrushes and warblers arrive as well. Ducks, too, are back, rafting up in the estuaries by the hundreds and thousands, feeding and resting before completing the last leg north. And the hooligan come in. Every nook of the natural world seems to have a phenomenon or two that only people familiar with the land know about. On the northwestern coasts hooligan - a soft, smelt-like fish - pour into the rivers in numberless formations, a crucial event. Animals all winter scrape by on the sparity of the land and the scraps of wolf-kills, when suddenly an endless line of easily-caught, oil-laden fish return to the waterways.

A few years ago I didn't know much about hooligan, or anything else in the area for that matter. I'd spent a couple summers in Alaska but had only lived there a full year when I had a week between jobs the first spring . It was early April, and I decided to paddle out of the little town where I live, initially on an extended estuary, then fifteen miles or so up a river, into the foothills of a considerable mountain chain. I didn't know how far I'd get, but gave myself the full week to see how it went.

I'd bought a canoe the previous fall and it's a beauty, designed, it seems, for going upstream. The air was crisp but the paddling warm. Clouds spit occasional rain, but overall things were pleasant the first day. The initial leg was simple, a five mile creek downstream to the estuary. About half way down I ran into the first hooligan, moving in great hordes, slow but steady, pressing upstream to spawn. Eagles were everywhere, dotted in the towering spruce. After a winter of semi-dormancy, the hooligan had restored them. Kingfishers, too, chatted and darted among the lower alders, and ravens - intelligent, weird in the old way - communicated their strange language from the trees and the air.

Steering the canoe along the stream's lazy turns my eyes rested mostly on the metallic fish. As individuals they struggled mightily. As a group they were unstoppable. Scores of corpses, stiff and drained of color, gathered in the sandy, gentle eddies along the bottom. Others, near death, succumbing to exhaustion, swirled here and there in dazed circles. In the main, though, the juggernaught was unfazed. Over on the bank, yards away, I heard a great huff, then what I thought was a familiar sound. I looked up. Having forgotten where I was, I expected to see a horse cantering away. It wasn't. A brown bear, lithe and worn from hibernation, sped across the open bank toward the brush. I'd seen them before, but never so close and never so well. For a few strides every muscle was visible, throbbing and huge beneath thick flesh and thicker fur. I understood then why they tell you not to run. It wasn't the first time I'd felt humbled and puny in the woods, but it was the first time

I felt utter vulnerability before a single creature. Like the birds, it too had come down for the hooligan.

When I got to the estuary the tide had just turned, carrying me along the wide water paralleling the shore. A spare, dark sandy spit blocked the ocean, but the acoustics of the gentle breakers outside crept over the bar. By now I was miles from town. I'd been alone in the woods countless times, but this was different. Behind me, westward, lay the village, three hours by canoe, while yards to the south rolled the Pacific. To the north and east was river and forest, flat beneath the mountains, peopleless for two hundred miles or more.

Even with a tide, paddling a canoe takes time. Still, stroke after stroke, you plod along, marking progress. Beyond a long island, where the river split, a smaller creek joined the estuary. About here the tide stopped and I started pushing against current. This area is known as the flats, a long series of ever-changing sandbars and shifting channels. The land and water track on such a plane as to make mirages common, where what is sand and what is water is indistinguishable even at close distances. Without the occlusion of the tide, the hooligan were notice-able again, and in far greater numbers than before. Every stroke of the paddle knocked a couple dozen out of formation, opening a space until they recovered. Birds were here, too, ducks at first. Pintails, scaup, teal, and mallards - all gathered in mixed flocks. They never let me close, having from Alaska to Mexico and back to Alaska learned that my kind hunts their kind with startling vigor.

It was around here that I heard, then saw, the first seal. A deep-throated splash sounded behind me. I turned and looked, seeing nothing but a widening swirl. A few strokes later and they were all around, a couple dozen or more. Like everything else, the hooligan are a great boon to them. They follow the multitudes into the river mouths then up toward the shallows, by turns gorging themselves and hauling out in great pods upon the sandbars. I'd paddled right into a frenzy. Several came close to the boat, their enormous, curious black eyes regarding whatever they saw before them. As each surfaced it let out a loud breath, like a pipe bursting under pressure. They did this repeatedly, bobbing in a staggered circle around the boat, making an odd staccato. After a while, though, they lost interest. I kept paddling, and soon the last of them was behind me.

There's a vitality to mirage light. The horizon seems blurred, jittering slightly in varied textures. For a moment, a quarter mile past the seals, I thought the flats were covered in snow. Acres were blanched in quivering whites. I hadn't, though, noticed the sound. Seagulls, thousands of them, stood on the sandy banks or floated together in the coursing water, squealing away, each taking what must have been their first easy meals in months. I was a few hundred yards from the main body. A ragged line - much closer - led up to it. The first of these took off, then another, then many more in succession. Soon the whole group spooked, several thousand birds lifting at once, making great fuss and commotion. After the initial confusion, though, a decisive direction was chosen, directly at me. For a moment the explosion of such energy after miles of quietude left me motionless. As they drew nearer, however, I knew what was going to happen. My raincoat was draped over the canoe's yoke, and I rushed to put it on as the first gulls flew over. I pulled the hood over my head, knelt on the bottom, and tucked my bare hands into my body. Like a summer squall, the first drops hit sporadically but thick and hard, followed by the deluge. All I could do was hunch down. For thirty seconds the droppings hit my back and the boat indiscriminately, and the absurdity of it, indignity even, caught me and I broke out laughing, still curled into myself. When the popping on the water stopped I looked up. The birds were over the beach by then.

Laughing is peculiar, a highly social phenomenon. We don't do it much when we're alone. When we do, it accentuates the solitude. No one was there to see it, and I realized the laugh wouldn't be complete until I returned home and recounted it. Still, I didn't mind. That day wasn't far off. I beached the boat and gave everything a thorough scrub-down - my gear, my jacket, the boat - then paddled the remainder of the estuary, turning, eventually, north toward the mountains, somewhere miles ahead through the shifting fogs.

I camped twice on the way up. In a canoe you can make about a mile an hour upstream. With twelve hours of daylight, that gave me nine hours of comfortable traveling time. The first night, with daylight just starting to fade, I pitched the tent on a high bank covered in willow and alder in a crescent-shaped clearing not much bigger than the tent itself. Next I gathered wood. Fires aren't always possible in a rain forest but it hadn't come down hard lately and if you look for dead branches on the still-living trees enough dry wood can usually be found. I'd brought enough food but with the hooligan there for the taking I decided to conserve. Wading in, I plucked a dozen or so from the cold river. On the opposite bank, a mink loped beneath the dangling brush, slipping into the current and coming out with a fish of its own. Otter tracks covered the sandbars around me, their scaly scat left among the clumsy foot-prints. On one bar a larger set of prints - a brown bear's - blotted out those of the otters.

Hooligan smoke well but other than that are quite bland, even mealy. Still, you never seem to eat much when camping and if nothing else the oil was welcome. I hung the other food and some gear in one of the few spruce along the lower river, pulled the canoe on the bank, then cracked a book by the dying fire. All day in a canoe wears you down, though, and I didn't last long. When I rose a beaver startled in the river below, slapping its tail against the water before diving beneath. I wondered if anything else out there heeded the warning. I went to the tent, put a loaded shotgun by my side, then slipped inside the sleeping bag. Outside I heard nothing. It's rare, nowadays, to fall asleep in total darkness and total silence, and quite pleasant. I woke many hours later, still in silence, with the first, steely glow of day gloaming through the tent fabric.

That day was a travel day. I figured if I had a shot at getting near the mountains I needed a lot of miles before nightfall. The canoe was loaded before full light. I hadn't had much experience paddling up a river, but the logic is simple. Running water is mostly a continuum of pools and riffles. Riffles are usually shallow and better to walk through, while most pools have an eddy of some sort, either reversing or neutral-izing the current. It doesn't take long to find the easiest routes, and after a while the rhythm of walking and paddling, paddling and walking, becomes ruminative, with abstract thought partitioning the conscious mind from physical labor, making the latter nearly involuntary. I scared a moose around one bend, who'd been crossing the stream on a shallow gravel bar. It panicked, wheeling around and angling upstream to the other bank, a foolish move. The water deepened here and in a few strides he was in over his head, swimming. I stopped mid-river, alternating the paddle from side to side to keep the boat steady. The moose had picked a place too steep to climb, and after a few frantic attempts slipped clumsily into the current, where it regained traction in the gravel. Standing, it assessed me for a minute or more before recovering its composure. I was in deep water myself and didn't worry. It began moving in the unrhythmic, lumbering strides of its breed, then crossed on the original route, ascending the bank in a crash of brush and motion. When we're outside nature we think of it fondly as a place where everything jibes in harmony. It isn't. Animals - like us - err all the time. I paddled forward and got out to walk over the bar where the creature had crossed. Absent of fanfare the river I now moved through would swallow either me or that moose if we let it without any thought that we're aware of.

Clouds had thickened over the day and instead of rain a thick, oatmealish snow came down. It clung to everything in the boat and as it melted filled the bottom with slush and water, spoiling the ballast. Every half mile or so I pulled ashore, emptying the gear and turning over the canoe. That night I camped in a thick spruce grove, where the heavy trees trap enough heat to leave the ground wet but clear. I didn't attempt a fire, spending most of the dwindling daylight stringing tarps and stowing gear in such a way as to keep everything dry. Sleep came easily, and I again woke at first light.

By dawn, five inches of new snow had covered the gravel bars and open banks, adding to the old patches that in places remained three feet deep. After loading the canoe I took a moment and looked in the pool at my feet, noticing something I hadn't the previous day. The hooligan were gone. Downstream somewhere, in the prolonged reveries common to solitude and physical exertion, I'd paddled above their range. Looking up, I found something else. I'd gone much farther than I thought. The clouds had broken slightly during the night, and between strips of fog I saw mountains, larger and much closer than expected. By mid-day I'd made it, not to the mountains themselves - mostly barren and packed in year-round snow - but to the foothills, which if not large are lush with timber and other life.

Like all rivers this one changes character closer to its source. The grade is steeper and the water shallower. The land in southeast Alaska is also rapidly expanding, as the glacial till of its many rivers spills out into the ocean ton after ton, adding to the beaches. The further inland you go, then, the older the land, a fact reflected in the vegetation. Here, upriver, spruce dominated the banks, marking the ground's older age. There's not much soil for them to root into, and as such they're highly susceptible to wind and floods. Subsequently, on the way up, log jams dotted the river. Some were simple, merely popping the canoe over a single timber, while others were more detailed, involving unloading everything and portaging around through the snow and the brush. Throughout the morning the clouds broke up, as well, leaving blue sky, sunlight, and the increasingly larger figures of the mountain chain looming ahead.

Up here choices were necessary. Smaller streams and branches make large rivers what they are, and several similar-sized creeks conjoined at varying spots, forcing decisions. There are maps of this area, and good ones, but not so detailed to delineate every tributary. As I picked my way I wondered how many people had made these same choices. Starting a century ago, natives probably made them all the time. More recently, it receives less traffic. Cartographers and biologists have made forays in here, but not in earnest for a couple decades or more, and every couple years or so a bear hunter will head up this way on a day trip. Other than that, it's clean. I picked what I thought were the straightest routes to the closest hills, realizing now that no one really knew where I was nor cared what decisions I made. Certain brands of solitude, then, engender unique degrees of freedom and oppression alike.

The last stream was little more than a hop-across affair, opening up from spruce forest to an enormous, willow-laden muskeg abutting the foothills. It looked like beaver country and it was. Dams new and old clogged the creek, along with the many rivulets feeding it. Beavers are the great woodland providers wherever they go. The ponds attract every resident creature, who come to feed either on the thick vegetation that itself feeds on the swampy ground, or upon other creatures. Pulling the canoe over one dam - a jumble of whittled willow limbs and mortared mud - a great canine print remained in a faded patch of snow. A wolf had been here. Salmon, too, who supply the bulk of nutrition to both plants and animals in this country, are greatly aided by beavers. Juveniles thrive in the ponds, with the deep, dark water offering fine refuge from predators, while the nutrient-rich waters provide better than usual fodder. Spring time is smolting time for them, and clouds of thumb-long fish - their bodies rapidly changing in preparation for the ocean - darted to cover from time to time as I passed over them. Mergansers, too - common and hooded - spooked at my approach. They were here for the gathering fish, as I'd imagined their ancestors had been centuries ago. As spring went on, and the smolt began their migration, the birds would follow, hounding them to the sea. The mountains, even though still miles away, lorded over me now in bright sunlight and gleaming snow-pack. Nearer, only a few hundred yards away, the first spruce-covered hillocks lay. I paddled until the stream grew too narrow for the boat, then got out to find a camping spot. The sun was still high, and there was time to find a good one.

After pulling the boat on the bank, I headed for the first elevation, more a hummock than a hill. The sun beat down on the muskeg, and I could see much dry wood in the standing willow. The dams here were old and worn through, but they'd left strips of dead willow standing behind them which the sunlight now worked upon. I kept moving. As the ground gradually rose, the willow gave way to blueberry then the first spruce. At the base of the hillock, nestled between two large evergreens, draped in lichen, a deep spring bubbled from the ground, the pumping water gently roiling the pool's dark surface. It spilled over the back to form a substantial springlet running by my feet. I headed up the incline, passing through the spiny devil's club and over windfalls. The top wasn't more than a hundred yard climb.

The peak was actually three peaks, several soft summits split by gentle valleys. One of these was flat and soft and I cleared a little vegetation away before returning to the boat for the gear. Humping it back, I strung tarps and pitched the tent, then made several trips up and down to the muskeg, carrying as much dead willow as I could each time. The high-pressure system that had brought the sun also dropped the temperature and it looked to be a chilly night. A couple hours' daylight remained after camp was set, and I walked the narrow stream I'd paddled up, where a bear trail made the bush-whacking tolerable. No bear tracks, though, were here, as most of the animals were either still denned-up or down near the river mouth, chasing hooligan. Signs of them, however - old ones - were present. Snow melts spottily at times. In places it was four feet deep, while in other patches the ground was bare - soft, soggy stretches of bank, covered in moss and flattened grass.

In these the remains of salmon from the previous fall were everywhere - jaw bones, gill plates, spinal columns - strewn about like eroded fossils. The bears are here at that time, having followed the fish to their spawning grounds, where salmon are simple to catch in the shallow, oxygen-rich riffles they need to lay eggs. Bears often only eat the brains, leaving the rest for the jays, mink, ravens, and other opportunists. By the end, only scattered bones remain, every year leaching their sea-borne particles to the young and burgeoning forest. Life now, though, was certainly more than remnant here. In the dark, tannic waters fry and smolt moved beneath the overhangs at my approach, themselves beneficiaries of the nutrients the dying adults bequeath every season to the young of their kind. The little fish now at my feet would return one day to do the same. Out over the ocean, far away, the sun dropped quickly, merging with the horizon in a deep, uniform orange. I turned, walking the same trail back to camp.

The fire started easily. Wood rarely gets completely dry here but this stuff was close. Through the spruce canopy stars sparkled in every gap. Other than the gentle crackling in the fire, the woods were still, at least to my senses. I couldn't see, hear, or smell a thing. That, though, didn't mean much. Out there, in blackness, mink chased balls of smolt in the beaver ponds, while saw-whet owls and great-horned's kept their vigils for the hares and voles, who worked cautiously through the underbrush, sensing the greenery soon to come. Wolves, too, in packs or alone, hunted the foothills and muskegs, looking for everything from moose to mice. A weak column of smoke made it's way skyward in the glow of the fire. I was strange in this place, and whatever scents I threw off were no doubt received by the creatures who lived here.

There was no need to move the next day. The camp was comfortable and there was more territory here than I could cover in a month. Besides, after the long days of paddling a respite sounded nice. I woke early to another clear, crisp morning, and after reviving the fire and having a little breakfast, walked over to the adjacent summit and looked on the other side of the hill, where a long, narrow muskeg spread out of the bottom before rising immediately into larger mountains. The sun had ascended by now and was warming up the flat ground below me. I put some lunch in a day pack, then picked my way downslope through the spruce to the swampy ground below.

The muskeg took some doing. I'd left my waders in camp, happy to be in rubber boots after two days of confinement. This side of the hill, though, had active beaver dams. With the brush and the deeper waters, then, I had to take a more careful route. Right along the mountains ran a wide, shallow, stony creek, and the signs of last year's salmon were thicker than before. Bones lay atop bones in places, and the deep pits in the stream gravel showed where the fish had labored to construct a place for their eggs. Mink scat rested on several spots along the banks, and a large, matted pile of fish scales showed where otters had made a toilet months ago. Crossing on an ankle-deep bar, I found a considerable bear trail on the other bank, curving along with the contour of the mountain chain. Bears are known for stepping in the same spots year after year, generation after generation, and in several flat stretches the trail was marked by a dozen of more of these ancestral footfalls.

A mile or so down I picked the gentlest incline I could find and started climbing. These hills weren't terribly large either, and I doubt this one rose a thousand feet. Thick blueberry and devil's club, though, growing amongst many fallen spruce, slowed the climb somewhat. Dense and encompassing, the standing timber fractured the sun in thick shards that hit the mossy ground at all angles. On two occasions I could hear a flock of kinglets chipping in the needles high above, but never saw the diminutive shapes. Several boulders, huge and out of place in a land with little bedrock, were strewn sporadically about the slope, where the glaciers had dumped them centuries ago on their way back into the mountains. One of these, erect and narrow, had fissured atop the little mountain and stood at the peak like a rent steeple. When I reached these I could see the mountains now, clear and unobstructed.

We forget how much of the earth is unavailable to us, even the dry land. Before me was little more than rock and snow, stacked in violent elevation. Compared to the hump where I stood, the mostly nameless mountains behind it were sharp, jagged peaks softened below by glacier-worn valleys. Timber was scarce. A few trees clung to the lower elevations, but were dwarves compared to the ranging specimens I'd just walked through. The land, then, was too new, too austere, too beat-up by ice to support much life. In three different passes I could see glaciers rumpled up in the distance, still-to-the-eye but active all the same.

Here, as in most of the world, they're in full retreat. I'd looked at maps before I'd come out. These particular glaciers were probably in Canada. I sat against one of the rocks and rested, while a Stellar's Jay, agile and deft, regarded me from several branches, keeping silent as it hopped and fluttered to its various perches. The lands that are so useful to us now - the Plains, much of the northwest, the still-productive farmland of the mid-Atlantic - all at one time or another benefited from the shape-shifting power of ice. One day the stingy glacier and rock before me would as well settle into gentle fertility, but that was thousands of years off. I wondered if names like Canada and the United States would be in living memories by then, or if human beings would even be around. The jay let out a cat's mew, flicked its wings, then sailed downslope in the direction of the ice. I turned, picked my way back down the hill, walked the trail again, then crossed the muskeg back to camp.

I re-watered at the spring, filling two plastic jugs. As the sun died I read a book atop the over-turned canoe, then went up the hill to re-kindle the fire. The stars again peered through the spruce, and once more no creature made itself known. As in each of the nights, sleep came soon and deep. The next morning I woke early and headed down river.

By the time the canoe was loaded, the sun, rising steadily behind the peaks, pushed more and more light out over the land. The grass in the muskeg had crystallized over night, crunching beneath my feet as I worked to prepare the boat. When the vessel was in the creek, facing oceanward, I stopped to enjoy the silence. The mountains - a blackened outline not long ago - gained color and relief in the increasing light, and soon the sun appeared, a thin ribbon of orange peering between two peaks. It's impossible to say what makes such things. I know just enough of tectonics and friction and other principles to know how land-scapes are formed, but what put it all in motion is beyond me, beyond everyone. The sun, rising steadily above the chain, was up now. All of it - the mountains, the glaciers, the ground beneath me - was moving all the time, but if I stood there the rest of my life I'd never notice it. If a human being stood where I stood for the next thousand years none of us together would notice it. Something, though, does, and it's in this way that nature edifies us. If it doesn't give us the answers, it puts us in direct contact with the questions. I stepped in the canoe, took my seat, and pushed off, taking my time over the next couple days on the way back to town.

I needed industry to make that trip. Oil was prominent, as was coal. The canoe was spun from petroleum and the spinning powered by coal fire. The bags that kept everything dry were spun from oil, too. The paddle was made of eastern ash, and all of it was trucked from Maine to Washington, then put on a barge for Alaska. Humans have always relied on research, industry, innovation, and development and we always will. It powers, sustains, and makes possible our survival. If we relied on chipped stones and bent sticks ten thousand years ago, we rely on steel, combustion, and plastic today. We have, though, according to both the sentiment and personal common sense of most of us, reached the point where balance is needed. Intelligence is humanity's only viable asset, but it's a formidable force. We'll have to wield it, now, toward equilibrium, coming up with new, less invasive means of production while reigning in our thirst for both material acquisition and land development. Whether it's done inside or outside government is irrelevant. Likely, it'll take both. Government can - more so than it's currently doing - encourage cleaner innovations through example and incentive. Individually, we can all strive to find the balance that Teddy Roosevelt and many others envisioned long ago. As most people know, we - particularly Americans - buy a great deal of unnecessary items. Even a little discipline in this regard will make giant strides collectively. Energy vigilance, as well, is crucial. No one wants the government telling them when and why they have to walk rather than ride a car, or demand that they turn the lights off when they leave a room, and government shouldn't have to decree these things, as common sense does that. A mile isn't far to walk, and it's good for you besides. Light isn't necessary when you're not in a room, and it sucks a great deal of energy. When the bulk of individuals make decisions like this on their own, a healthy equality between consumption and conservation may be struck. If not, then nature - the last of it - will be lost, and with it the forum in which the best part of ourselves resides.

Chapter 16

Conclusion

We all want the world to go our way. Our love of compromise, therefore, is more in line with utility than desire, and concession a mark of pragmatism rather than nobility. How this country will turn out, then, I have no idea, but if I could will it my way I know the direction I'd want it to take.

Much of that direction has to do with standard ideology. A great portion of our country's promise pertains to both individual merit and happiness, unfettered by the meddling of prejudice and amplified by the boon of equality. As such, I - like the majority - would like to see the continued creep in the generational mitigation of racism coincide with the constant reform and upkeep of quality education for all people. If such progress comes to fruition, as it should, then pre-judgement and imbalance will be banished to whatever low levels we inherit through nature, and the country will surge as a result. Like much ideological ambition, however, such forward movement is more a function of time, patience, and the subtle shifts within individuals, families, and communities than it is the spawn of legislation. This motion takes generations, and most of the change I desire fits this description.

Government, of course, plays its role. In fact, it's often instrumental in fostering such change. We live under the rule of law, afterall, and are therefore shaped by laws themselves. If the country has benefited from the painfully slow decay of raw racism in the years since Appomattox, that decay was certainly spurred by congressional landmarks such as the Fourteenth Amendment and Civil Rights legislation. In kind, the steady awakening to the environmental consequences of modern life can point to bills passed in the seventies as a primary mover. Laws in a free country, though, are a reflection of natural movements within the populace, and can only facilitate those same movements' maturity. The genesis of such inertia occurs in the thoughts and emotions of individuals, and it's here where change finds its greatest drive. Government - if it's doing its job - merely responds to such movement. Subsequently, in the very near future I'd like to see a few general shifts in the popular will.

Abroad, I'd want the recent fervor many Americans have toward restructuring the globe through warfare severely ruptured. If this is a liberal aim, it's heavily buttressed by conservative tenets. George H.W. Bush cheered the Gulf War's overturning of the 'Vietnam Syndrome', a cheering which has since taken an uncomfortably firm hold, particularly since the fall of the twin towers. For me, and many like me, 9/11 may have changed the world but it didn't change it that much. Vietnam's resonance is a lesson, not a syndrome. Not only does it still hold sway but should be heeded in today's climate. People don't like being invaded for any reason, and will - as any American would - fight with everything they have to oust that invasion, producing a long, costly war which is at best partially successful. Nation-building only works when the population at large is not only defeated but feels - from children to grandmothers - the impending doom of cultural and physical annihilation. Germany and Japan felt it and capitulated unconditionally. Ambiguity, however, was entirely absent then. Vietnam was - and Iraq is - suffused with uncertainty, rendering annihilation nearly unthinkable. Supplanting back alley dictators that we've supported heavily in the past doesn't make for an unflinching, unified decision to destroy a nation and its people, which is the only way a conquered populace will ever fully comply with reconstruction. Sometimes - very seldomly - such destructive resolve is necessary and happens naturally, as in World War II. Short of that, I'd very much like the vast majority of this country to return to the fundamental American principle of leaving the world to its own affairs when it comes to military involvement. If we haven't always lived this way, it remains our natural penchant, and one we should abide in most cases. When we do interfere, it should only be with the express intent of total war, in a commitment entirely absent of moral incertitude.

If people are a mixture of liberal and conservative material, the preponderance of one or the other exists just the same. Occasionally a single event will reveal that preponderance clearly, and 9/11 - if it was nothing else - was such an event. Like half the nation's, my reaction was purely liberal. When faced with a conflict - any conflict - it's liberal orthodoxy to ask what you yourself may have contributed to the problem. To me this makes the most sense. You have the most control over your own actions than of any other thing in the world, particularly global politics. Concerning the recent Muslim violence against the West, all but the blind and insane acknowledge that American and European intrusions into Middle Eastern sovereignty are at very least a contributing factor to that rage and the begrudging support of Islamic fundamentalists that causes it. Oil, of course, is the sole issue driving those intrusive policies, and as a consumer of it I have to come to terms with my own contributions to the violence now at hand. If I can't change geopolitics, I can at least recognize my minute effects upon them and try to live a sounder, less abusive life as an individual, in this case becoming more aware of the consequences my actions and decisions may produce.

Investing both pervasive power and responsibility in the individual, of course, is also high on the conservative docket. The difference, at least in theory, is that whereas individual liberal power is more reactive conservatives are more active. What's actual and not actual, however, isn't my concern. If I could, though, realize for the future a blend of the two, I'd do it with the wave of a hand. Were I granted the power to form a governing ethos of the American majority within the next generation it would be of a people fully aware of individual sovereignty, coupled with the willingness to accept, cherish, and exercise it. Rather than resign environmental, social, or economic tribulations to globalization or corporate power structures, they'd realize what they themselves could do to combat such forces - largely through purchasing and lifestyle decisions - and improve their own lives that way. In short, frugality would trump frivolity as the dominant American trait. Additionally, they'd be people who understand fully that Western behavior in the last century largely led to present-day bloodshed. If they - like me - don't care for or even comprehend how other cultures live their lives - most particularly in China or the Middle East - they'll also understand that what happens over there isn't the province of America to alter by force. The best thing we can do is live life how we choose to live it, and if others want to follow that's their choice, not ours.

Above all things, perhaps, I'd like to see in the coming years a sweeping dedication to environmental stewardship, for the physical - if not the spiritual and psychological - sake of all people. Rather than bickering over what if any contribution humans have made to the undeniable global warming trend, individuals inside and outside government will concentrate on the more tangible consequences that the unbridled, sloppy consumption of resources has upon human health. Flicking on central air, in other words, comes with a price, and people need to understand that if conditions are to improve. Conversely, extreme environmentalists must acknowledge that minerals need to be mined, timber felled, and oil drilled, but with a collective awareness that such practices can be both cleaned up and lessened through greater economy in individual use and the drive to find other, equally reliable energies. When such cognizance predominates in the populace, it will be reflected in the government as a matter of course.

If this new generation chooses to wrap themselves in the American flag during every conversation, they'll know fully what that flag means, good things and bad. Our country has a fairly lengthy history by now and people should know it entirely. On the other hand, if others choose to criticize America, they'll be aware of the many things the nation has done well, both past and present. The concept of god will be left to where it's most liberated and productive, the privacy of worship and theological discussions, and completely left out of both scientific inquiry and the halls of congress. Lastly, people will understand the mixture - or marbling - in both themselves and everyone else. Stereotypes of leftists as ivory tower elitists and right-wingers as Christ-bitten warmongers will be reserved for comedy sketches, not serious analysis. There's a little bit of everything in all of us, and if compromise isn't our first choice in the individual ideal, it remains our most practical, decently-directed tool for everyone to get the most of what they want. Voting, of course, remains paramount. For my own part, whether it's Democrat, Republican, or the emergence of a new party, I'll in the future free myself to choose the people most in line with my beliefs, understanding that in a country of free flowing ideas built on compromise perfect candidates don't exist.

www.ingramcontent.com/pod-product-compliance
Lightning Source LLC
LaVergne TN
LVHW042153230325
806687LV00030B/309